Good Friends

Relationships & Faith

LEADER'S GUIDE

Tim Gossett

Abingdon Press

Good Friends
Relationships & Faith
LEADER'S GUIDE

Copyright © 2002 by Abingdon Press.

This book is printed on acid-free, recycled paper.

Unless otherwise noted, Scripture quotations are from the *New Revised Standard Version of the Bible,* copyright © 1989, Division of Christian Education of the National Council of the Churches of Christ in the United States of America. Used by permission. All rights reserved.

03 04 05 06 07 08 09 10 11—10 9 8 7 6 5 4 3 2

MANUFACTURED IN THE UNITED STATES OF AMERICA

Development Team
Jola Bortner
Rusty Cartee
Harriette Cross
Tim Gossett
Sharon Meads
Beth Miller
David Stewart

Editorial Team
Crystal A. Zinkiewicz, Senior Editor
Pam Shepherd, Production Editor

Design Team
Keely J. Moore, Design Manager
Kelly Chinn, Designer

Administrative Staff
Neil M. Alexander, Publisher
Harriett Jane Olson, Vice President/Editor of Church School Resources
Bob Shell, Director of Youth Resources

CONTENTS

How to Use Faith in Motion

Leader Guide
Information and Formation

Topic and Key Verse
This Life-to-Bible curriculum starts with important topics for junior highs and goes to God's Word.

Take-Home Learning
The goal for the session is clear.

Younger Youth and the Topic
Find out more about your youth and how they are likely to connect with this concern.

Theology and the Topic
How does Christian faith and tradition help us to understand and deal with the concern?

You and the Scripture
Our being formed as a Christian through Bible reflection and prayer is essential for our teaching.

SESSION 1

My Crazy, Mixed-up family

Topic: Improving Family Relationships

Scripture: 1 John 3:11-20

Key Verse: "Little children, let us love, not in word or speech, but in truth and action." (1 John 3:18)

Take—Home Learning: Families come in many different shapes and sizes, and none of them are perfect. Teens can positively influence their family lives through their actions and attitudes.

Younger Youth and This Topic

You can be certain of at least one thing concerning families of the youth you teach: There is no one model of what a family looks like in today's society. Families can be nuclear (husband and wife), single parent, extended (grandparents or others living in the same house), step, foster, adoptive, and group or communal. Only about forty-seven percent of the millennial generation will experience life with two parents who live in the same home—the traditional family is no longer the norm. Every form of family has its inherent advantages and disadvantages, and they are far too numerous to list. However, there are two important similarities.

First, while younger youth often claim that their families are crazy and mixed up, they have grown up believing their individual families are normal. If a family is vegetarian, vegetarian is normal (for them). If a family is dysfunctional, then dysfunctional is normal. Younger youth often compare their families to those of their friends. While they may like some things about their friends' families, ultimately their particular family structure feels most normal to them.

Second, whatever communication patterns exist in their families are perceived by them as normal. If communication in the family is good, teens assume that's how a family should communicate. If, however, there is poor

Eighteen percent of Millennials, the current generation, will be raised by an unmarried parent. Thirty-five percent will experience their parents' divorce.
—Craig Kennet Miller.

From YouthNet © 1999 The United Methodist Publishing House.

Theology and the Topic

Given all the talk in Christian circles about the "Christian home," one might assume that a clear biblical image exists for what a family should look like. Few model families appear in the Bible, especially in the New Testament. In fact, the Bible offers many accounts of families who went beyond being dysfunctional to being downright deadly. How would you like to have been part of Adam and Eve's family, Isaac and Rebekah's family, Gideon's family, Jephthah's family, or Zebedee's family?

Indeed, biblical families are a lot like soap-opera families—full of passion one day and anger the next. Why? Probably because the business of keeping a family together is attempted by flawed individuals and is hard work. If the "first family" of Scripture—who embodied the biblical values of God in their relationships—had difficulty succeeding as a family, should we be surprised that so many families today have troubles? Regardless of how hard we try, parents and siblings can only love with an imperfect love—because none of us are perfect.

The family is the best "Love Learning Laboratory" you'll ever experience. Where else can one consistently learn and practice the biblical values of kindness, trust, patience, nurture, compassion, and more? If we believe that God is love (1 John 4:8), we don't have to invite God into our homes. Because of that belief, God is already there and experienced through our relationships with one another.

You and the Scripture

A boy and his father were walking along a road when they came across a large stone. The boy said to his father, "Do you think if I use all my strength, I can move this rock?" His father answered, "If you use all your strength, I am sure you can do it." The boy began to push the rock. Exerting himself as much as he could, he pushed and pushed. The rock did not move. Discouraged, he said to his father, "You were wrong. I can't do it." His father placed his arm around the boy's shoulder and said, "No, son. You didn't use all your strength—you didn't ask me to help."

Sometimes our families' actions offer us a glimpse of the type of love God has for us. And sometimes we forget that when loving others is truly difficult, we probably aren't using all our strength. When we allow God's love to abide in us, God's call in our lives becomes doable.

- When did you first hear the message that we should love one another? (verse 11) How has your understanding of love changed over time?

- When have you been hated, put down, or rejected because you chose the way of love? (verse 13) How did you feel?

- In what ways have you set aside your own life for the lives of others? (verse 16) When is this most difficult for you to do?

Read 1 John 3:11-20.

Pray for the families of the youth in your class. Pray that their families might be a window through which the youth see and feel God's love.

8

Good Friends

Transformation

The ultimate goal: Youth will become more fully devoted disciples of Jesus Christ.

Overview Chart
Look here for the big picture of the session. Also note the key activities, just in case time is tight.

Jump Right In!
The opening activity engages youth as they arrive.

Experience It!
Learning activities give youth a common base for making new connections.

Explore Connections
What do the Scriptures have to say? What does this mean for my life? What is a Christian to do?

Take the Challenge
The learnings are not just for Sunday!

Encounter the Holy
Ritual and mystery, prayer and commitment change hearts.

Student Journal and Reproducible Handouts

Life Focus
Topics deal with issues and concerns important to junior high youth.

Spirit Forming
The journal provides practical help and scriptural encouragement.

Group Friendly
Printed Scripture references, discussion questions, and handouts facilitate participation by individuals and small groups.

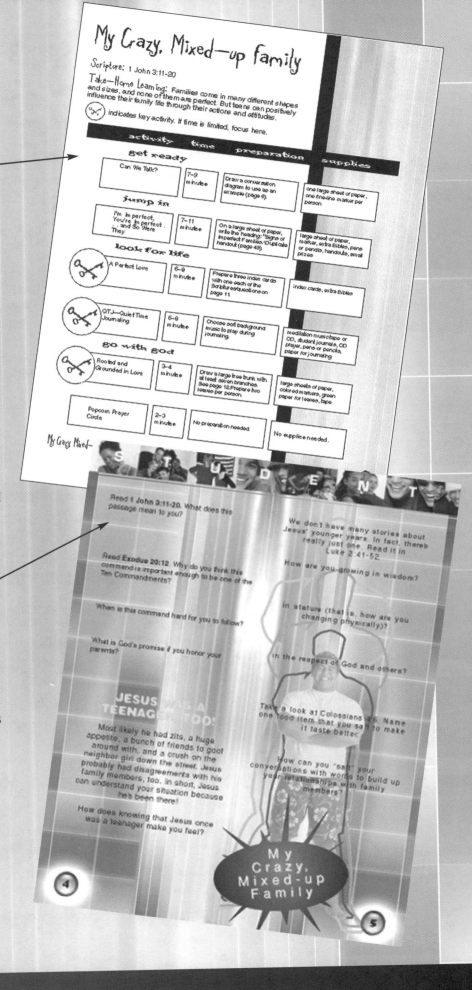

How Good a Friend Are You?

One of the most important things that happens in Sunday school
is deepening relationships between youth and their adult leaders.
Ask many a faithful Christian and they will say something like,
"I don't remember much about what I learned
from the lessons, but I do remember the teacher!"

That fact is not surprising. Ours is an *incarnational* (in the flesh) faith.
Think of Jesus; his life made God real to us! Our lives as faithful followers
of Christ help make God real to the young persons we teach. And often
they do the same for us!

Here's a quick self-test on building relationships and
being "the Bible youth see."

What's your body language?
Welcoming? approachable? interested?

Do you know them all by name?
Youth have a great need to be noticed and valued as unique individuals.

What do you know about each of them?
What are their Individual interests? their struggles? their gifts?

Do you talk to their families?
Are you passing on the positive?
Parents appreciate hearing good words.

Are you "instructing" or "sharing"?
Are you "the authority" or a "real person like me"?

How well do you listen?
Are you fully there? truly hearing? attending to what they share?

Of course, there will be times when you have to make energetic junior highs
"toe the line." And yes, you are teaching important truths and principles.
But you are also a mentor, encourager, representative of Christ, and *good friend!*

Blessings on you!

My Crazy, Mixed—up Family

Topic: Improving Family Relationships

Scripture: 1 John 3:11-20

Key Verse: "Little children, let us love, not in word or speech, but in truth and action." (1 John 3:18)

Take-Home Learning: Families come in many different shapes and sizes, and none of them are perfect. Teens can positively influence their family lives through their actions and attitudes.

Younger Youth and This Topic

You can be certain of at least one thing concerning families of the youth you teach: There is no one model of what a family looks like in today's society. Families can be nuclear (husband and wife), single parent, extended (grandparents or others living in the same house), step, foster, adoptive, and group or communal. Only about forty-seven percent of the millennial generation will experience life with two parents who live in the same home—the traditional family is no longer the norm. Every form of family has its inherent advantages and disadvantages, and they are far too numerous to list. However, there are two important similarities.

First, while younger youth often claim that their families are crazy and mixed up, they have grown up believing their individual families are normal. If a family is vegetarian, vegetarian is normal (for them). If a family is dysfunctional, then dysfunctional is normal. Younger youth often compare their families to those of their friends. While they may like some things about their friends' families, ultimately their particular family structure feels most normal to them.

Second, whatever communication patterns exist in their families are perceived by them as normal. If communication in the family is good, teens assume that's how a family should communicate. If, however, there is poor communication between family members, teens generally assume it is normal for parents and/or siblings to experience difficulties in getting along.

As you talk about families with class members, be sensitive to the many differences that exist. For example, be careful using phrases such as "your mom and dad" or "your brother or sister." These configurations may not apply to their situations. Also be aware that younger youth often complain about family members without attempting to find solutions to their complaints unless you help them. Discuss practical ideas to enhance family relationships, and point out ways to nurture bonding in any family.

Eighteen percent of Millennials, the current generation, will be raised by an unmarried parent. Thirty-five percent will experience their parents' divorce. —Craig Kennet Miller.

From *YouthNet,* © 1999 The United Methodist Publishing House.

Leaders Guide

My Crazy, Mixed-up Family

Theology and the Topic

Given all the talk in Christian circles about the "Christian home," one might assume that a clear biblical image exists for what a family should look like. Few model families appear in the Bible, especially in the New Testament. In fact, the Bible offers many accounts of families who went beyond being dysfunctional to being downright deadly. How would you like to have been part of Adam and Eve's family, Isaac and Rebekah's family, Gideon's family, Jephthah's family, or Zebedee's family?

Indeed, biblical families are a lot like soap-opera families—full of passion one day and anger the next. Why? Probably because the business of keeping a family together is attempted by flawed individuals and is hard work. If the "first family" of Scripture—who embodied the image of God in their relationships—had difficulty succeeding as a family, should we be surprised that so many families today have troubles? Regardless of how hard we try, parents and siblings can only love with an imperfect love—because none of us are perfect.

The family is the best "Love Learning Laboratory" you'll ever experience. Where else can one consistently learn and practice the biblical values of kindness, trust, patience, nurture, compassion, and more? If we believe that God is love (1 John 4:8), we don't have to invite God into our homes. Because of that belief, God is already there and experienced through our relationships with one another.

You and the Scripture

A boy and his father were walking along a road when they came across a large stone. The boy said to his father, "Do you think if I use all my strength, I can move this rock?" His father answered, "If you use all your strength, I am sure you can do it." The boy began to push the rock. Exerting himself as much as he could, he pushed and pushed. The rock did not move. Discouraged, he said to his father, "You were wrong. I can't do it." His father placed his arm around the boy's shoulder and said, "No, son. You didn't use all your strength—you didn't ask me to help."

Sometimes our families' actions offer us a glimpse of the type of love God has for us. And sometimes we forget that when loving others is truly difficult, we probably aren't using all our strength. When we allow God's love to abide in us, God's call in our lives becomes doable.

- When did you first hear the message that we should love one another? (verse 11) How has your understanding of love changed over time?

- When have you been hated, put down, or rejected because you chose the way of love? (verse 13) How did you feel?

- In what ways have you set aside your own life for the lives of others? (verse 16) When is this most difficult for you to do?

[1] TEACHING YOUR CHILDREN ABOUT GOD by David J. Wolpe, © 1993 by David J. Wolpe. Reprinted by permission of Henry Holt and Company, LLC.

Read **1 John 3:11-20.** Pray for the families of the youth in your class. Pray that their families might be a window through which the youth see and feel God's love.

Good Friends

My Crazy, Mixed—up Family

Scripture: 1 John 3:11-20

Take—Home Learning: Families come in many different shapes and sizes, and none of them are perfect. But teens can positively influence their family life through their actions and attitudes.

 indicates key activity. If time is limited, focus here.

activity	time	preparation	supplies
get ready			
Can We Talk?	7–9 minutes	Draw a conversation diagram to use as an example (page 8).	one large sheet of paper, one fine-line marker per person
jump in			
I'm Imperfect, You're Imperfect... and So Were They	7–11 minutes	On a large sheet of paper, write the heading: "Signs of Imperfect Families."Duplicate handout (page 49).	large sheet of paper, marker, extra Bibles, pens or pencils, handouts, small prizes
look for life			
A Perfect Love	6–8 minutes	Prepare three index cards with one each of the Scriptures/questions on page 11.	index cards, extra Bibles
QTJ—Quiet Time Journaling	6–8 minutes	Choose soft background music to play during journaling.	meditation music tape or CD, student journals, CD player, pens or pencils, paper for journaling
go with god			
Rooted and Grounded in Love	3–4 minutes	Draw a large tree trunk with at least seven branches. See page 12.Prepare two leaves per person.	large sheets of paper, colored markers, green paper for leaves, tape
Popcorn Prayer Circle	2–3 minutes	No preparation needed.	No supplies needed.

Get Ready

Provide one large piece of paper and fine-line marker per person. (If large paper is unavailable, use regular size.)

If possible, ahead of time, draw a diagram representing your own family's conversation patterns.

Jump In

Provide a large sheet of paper, marker, extra Bibles, You Think Your Family Is Weird? handouts (page 49), pencils, and small prizes.

On a large sheet of paper, write the heading, "Signs of Imperfect Families."

Answers: 1–Eve; 2–Jesus; 3–Noah; 4–John; 5–Jephthah's daughter; 6–the elder brother; 7–Rachel; 8–David; 9–Gideon; 10–daughter of Herodias

Can We Talk? (7–9 minutes)

Ask each youth to draw a rough sketch of the three rooms where most of the conversation occurs in his or her house. Encourage students to use their creativity to diagram some typical conversations that take place in those rooms. Suggest they use symbols such as triangles or Xs to represent individuals and to indicate the conversations in cartoon balloons. Share your own diagram as an example and discuss briefly.

After four to five minutes, ask teens to pair up with someone next to them and discuss the diagrams. Encourage students to identify any similarities in their diagrams.

After a few minutes of sharing, ask:
• What did you discover you had in common with your partner?
• Did you learn something new or gain a new insight about your own family?
• What types of conversations are most common in your home?

Say: "For the next several weeks, we will be looking at our relationships with family, friends, teammates, classmates, other adults, and God. Throughout all our conversations, one statement you may hear often is that the way we communicate with one another influences our relationships—good or bad. Our words reveal what is in our hearts and are indicators as to how we live out our faith in our relationships."

I'm Imperfect, You're Imperfect … and So Were They (7–11 minutes)

Say: "My guess is that in each of our families there is at least one area that feels crazy and mixed up. Let's list some signs of imperfect families."

Brainstorm as many examples as possible (about fifteen) of family disorder and dysfunction (arguing about rules, a parent who isn't home much, a rebellious sibling, and so forth).

Say: "That's a pretty representative list, and I'm sure we could add many other examples. Most of us can relate to at least one problem on the list. You might be surprised to find out there were troubled families in the Bible, too. In fact, it's tough to find examples of healthy families in the Scriptures.

Form small groups and give each group member a copy of the You Think Your Family Is Weird? handout (page 49) as well as Bibles and pencils.

Say: "On your handout are descriptions of Bible people who came from crazy, mixed-up families. The answers are listed in the margin in correct order. Each group's goal is to find the most correct answers in the fastest time. Check the Bible references listed beside each description. Write the answers below each statement." Team members may want to each take one reference. Encourage cooperation. (If teams are moving too slowly, you may want to post the answers in mixed-up order.)

When one group completes all the answers, reassemble as a large group. Review answers together. Consider awarding a small prize to the group with most correct answers.

Ask:
• Were any of the Bible stories unfamiliar to you?
• Are you surprised to discover so many crazy, mixed-up families in the Bible?
• Why do you think families are imperfect?

 ## A Perfect Love (6–8 minutes)

Say: "Your parents genuinely love you, but they love you with an imperfect love. Likewise, you love your family members with an imperfect love. That's why problems exist in our families. Still, we are called to grow in our love and to love as God loves. Let's study a Bible passage that speaks to this command.

Distribute Bibles to those who need them, and ask everyone to turn to 1 John 3:11-20. Call on a volunteer to read aloud the passage while everyone else follows along.

Form three groups. Assign each group one set of the questions below. Instruct groups to read the Bible passage and discuss questions for about a minute, then rotate the cards. After another minute, rotate the cards a third time so that each group discusses all of the questions.

1 John 3:14-15
• What does it mean if someone doesn't love as if she or he is dead?
• How can our words and actions be similar to murdering someone?

1 John 3:16-17
• What are some examples of ways we can "give up our lives" for family members?

1 John 3:18-20
• What does it mean to love someone with only your words?
• What does it mean to love your family with your actions?

After groups have talked about each set of questions, ask: "What does it mean to love others with the perfect love of God?"

 ## QTJ—Quiet Time Journaling (6–8 minutes)

Distribute Bibles, student journals, writing paper, and pens. Say: "Each week you'll have an opportunity to focus on our topic by journaling. Read pages 4 through 7 in the journal and follow the instructions there. If you need more space in which to write, I will give you extra sheets of writing paper. Fold them to fit inside your student journal. Write your thoughts about our topic for the day as it relates to your own families and other relationships.

My Crazy, Mixed-up Family

Look for Life

Provide extra Bibles and index cards.

Before the session, write each set of Bible passages and questions on separate index cards.

Provide Bibles, student journals, writing paper, pens, and soft background music.

"I will lock up the journals after each class; no one will see your journal but you. Don't worry about writing full sentences, spelling correctly, or giving the right answer. The point is to use this time to think about ways you can better show your love to family members."

Youth may either work in their seats, or spread out and find a private corner in which to write. Allow approximately five minutes for journaling. Also encourage youth to complete "This Week's Challenge" in the student journal (page 7). Play some soft, meditative background music. Collect journals at the end of class after checking for names.

Rooted and Grounded in Love (3–4 minutes)

Call attention to the tree trunk and roots. Say: "Each week we'll be adding leaves to our tree as a visual reminder of ways we can grow more like Jesus in our relationships." Distribute leaves, making sure each person receives at least two. Continue: "On one leaf, write one fact or truth you've learned today or one principle you think is important to remember about good relationships with our families." (Youth can add more than one leaf.) "Tape your leaves to the 'family' branch of the tree. As you attach your leaves, silently pray that God will help you with any problems you face in your family."

OR

Popcorn Prayer Circle (2–3 minutes)

Say: "We're going to conclude today with a Popcorn Prayer. I'll begin with a statement; at random, each of you can finish the statement with a prayer from your heart. Let's join hands."

Say: "Loving God, our heavenly parent, we thank you for these special members of our family." (Pause to allow responses.)

"We know that you call us to love and honor our families, yet we sometimes fall short. Forgive us for the times that we …" (Pause for responses.)

"With your help, God, our families can become a little less crazy and mixed up. Help us this week as we try to …" (Pause for responses.)

"We pray these things in Jesus' name, Amen."

Go With God

Provide large sheets of paper, markers, green construction paper, masking tape, leaf shape for tracing, and scissors.

Construct a tree using whatever supplies are available to you. For example, using a very large piece of paper, draw a tree trunk with seven branches. Or, you might collect seven real tree branches and nail to a post. Trace and cut out leaves using green paper; (Youth can do this step if necessary.) Write this verse on the roots: "May your roots go down deep into the soil of God's marvelous love" (Ephesians 3:17). On the trunk of the tree write "Me in Relationship to Others." On one of the branches write the word, "Family."

This activity will be an available option each week. If you choose the activity this week, plan to continue each week.

What Friends Are For

Topic: Having and Being a Great Friend

Scripture: Colossians 3:5-17

Key Verse: Above all, clothe yourselves with love, which binds everything together in perfect harmony. (Colossians 3:14)

Take—Home Learning: Friendships won't last without a firm foundation to keep them healthy and strong.

Younger Youth and This Topic

Teenagers' friends are like windows into their lives. To gain a greater understanding of the youth in your class, pay attention to their friendships. For younger youth, nearly everything in their lives revolves around their friends. For example, the first question most young teens ask about a church lock-in is not, "What are we going to do?" but "Who will be there?"

Learning to build and maintain friendships is one of the most important skills youth develop during their early teen years. They realize they don't always know how to initiate and nurture healthy friendships. So early adolescents will look to you for advice and listen to what you have learned and experienced. Communicate with them as a friend and not as one who only instructs them in the principles of friendship. If you truly want to help youth learn about friendship, involve yourself in their lives in whatever ways you can, ask about their interests and concerns, and make your classroom a welcoming and friendly place.

Remember—you can't pick friends for the teens in your class, nor can their parents. But you certainly can express your thoughts about the qualities of good friends, and you can offer youth a safe place to evaluate the quality of their friendships (often in an environment exclusive of their closest friends). Additionally, encourage your youth to build friendships with one another while in your class.

Theology and the Topic

"What a Friend We Have in Jesus," is a favorite hymn for many people. Perhaps it is because we all have experienced less than enduring friendships. In Jesus, we observe and encounter the ultimate example of friendship—one who was willing to lay down his life for his friends. The little word *for* is crucial: Friendship takes us to the heart of the Christian life, because true friendship isn't *for* any reason or purpose but the friend. People rarely experience the kind of deep friendship that isn't primarily about fulfilling one's own needs.

Sacramentalism means that anything can become a means of experiencing God's grace. We experience something of God in a rainbow, the leap of a frog, the smile of an infant, the kindness of a stranger, or a hug from a spouse. A friend's presence in your life is a grace, a sacramental sign that God loves you.

Friendships are also a primary way that teens—and adults—express devotion. Devotion is total dedication of our selves, a habit that extends through every act of our lives. The devotional practices of friendship, such as a weekly call to check on a friend who has moved to another state, help to feed our souls and empower us to grow spiritually. As we devote ourselves to the nurturing of our friendships, we also are nurtured, thus allowing us to again care for the needs of others.

You and the Scripture

Write the passage **Colossians 3:12-16** on another piece of paper (or the phrases you especially want to remember). Post it in your closet, medicine cabinet, or on a mirror where you'll read it each day.

• **"As God's chosen ones, holy and beloved."** We need to know we are loved by God before we love others. Do you see yourself as holy and beloved? What does this mean to you?

• **"Clothe yourselves with compassion, kindness, humility, meekness, and patience."** Do you ever wake up thinking to yourself, *What am I going to wear today?* Here's your daily answer: a choice that is up to you. Recall your interactions with friends and family during the past few days. How have your choices been representative of the "clothing" you chose to wear?

• **"Bear with one another ... forgive each other."** We all know people who are truly unbearable to be around. But with God's help, we can access the patience required to deal with them. We can discover an ability to forgive so that we can move forward as a loved and loving person. Who is hardest for you to be around? How have you practiced patience with them? Is there a need for forgiveness by you (in the same manner in which you are forgiven by God)?

• **"Let the word of Christ dwell in you richly."** What are you feeding your faith? Computer programmers recognize the phrase, "Garbage in, garbage out." Those things you allow into your heart, mind, and experience do shape you. What "health food for the soul" do you need to add to your life—Bible study, service, prayer, or other practice of faith—so that you can experience the indwelling of Christ?

Good Friends

What Friends Are For

Scripture: Colossians 3:5-17

Take—Home Learning: Friendships won't last without a firm foundation to keep them healthy and strong.

 indicates key activity. If time is limited, focus here.

activity	time	preparation	supplies
get ready			
"It's in the Cards"	6–8 minutes	Obtain carpet squares or textured fabric to use as bases for building if the room is not carpeted.	one deck of cards per group, carpet squares or textured fabric
jump in			
Friendship Killers and Keepers	7–9 minutes	Prepare a chart with two columns: Friendship Killers, Friendship Keepers.	large sheet of paper, marker, writing paper or student journals, pens or pencils
look for life			
Make It and Take It: Something to Stand On	5–8 minutes	Review "GROW" in the student journal (pages 10-11).	index cards in four different colors, markers, scissors, tape, student journals
E-Friendship	5–7 minutes	Cut small pieces of paper to distribute to students.	small pieces of paper and pens or pencils
QTJ—Quiet Time Journaling	7–9 minutes	Choose soft background music to play during journaling.	soft background music, student journals, pens or pencils
go with god			
Rooted and Grounded in Love and/or Connected	3–4 minutes	Prepare two green leaves for each person. On one of the branches, write the word, "Friends."	two green leaves per person, markers, tape

Get Ready!

Provide carpet squares or textured fabric and at least three decks of cards.

Tip: If the cards are not "cooperative," suggest to the youth it is OK to slightly bend the cards.

Jump In

Provide a large piece of paper, marker, writing paper, pencils, and student journals.

Draw a vertical line down the middle of a large piece of paper. Title one side, "Friendship Killers." Title the other side, "Friendship Keepers." Also use page 8 in the student journal.

Look for Life

Provide colored index cards, markers, and tape.

It's in the Cards (6–8 minutes)

As the youth arrive, form groups of three (one team may need to have either two or four persons). Give each group a deck of cards. Ask groups to move as far apart as possible. If the meeting room is not carpeted, give each group a carpet square or a piece of textured fabric as a base for building.

Say: "Work as a team to build a house of cards. Take turns in the group adding one or two cards at a time to the house. Each time you add a card, state one action/attitude/behavior that helps to build a friendship. You have about four minutes to build the strongest house you can. Go!"

After approximately four minutes, call time. Ask youth to compare their houses—strategies they used, problems they faced, and so on. Chances are, the strongest house will be the one with the firmest foundation. If no one mentions the foundation, ask: "What is the most important part of a house of cards?"

 ## Friendship Killers and Keepers (7–9 minutes)

Say: "Just as there are particular items that can help to strengthen a house of cards or cause it to fall, there are actions and attitudes that can build or hurt a friendship."

Ask:
• What are some actions/attitudes that can destroy a friendship? (List these items in the "Friendship Killers" column.)
• What are some behaviors or habits that can nurture growth in a friendship? (List these items in the "Friendship Keepers" column.)

Say: "Let's take a look at a Bible passage that relates to our lists." Form two groups (or several smaller groups if your class is large). Ask one group to read and discuss Colossians 3:5-11; ask the other to read and discuss Colossians 3:12-17. Provide each group with paper and pencils, or distribute the student journals.

Say: "Read your assigned passage, and note any items from Scripture that can be added to the "Friendship Killers/Keepers" list. Also identify reasons the actions or behaviors revealed in the passage fit in either of the categories." Allow two to three minutes for group work, then ask someone from each group to report. Add group findings to the list.

Make It and Take It: Something to Stand On (5–8 minutes)

Give each participant four index cards. If possible, provide cards in a variety of colors, and allow youth to choose colors. Also provide markers on each table. Say: "We have talked about the importance of a strong foundation when building a house of cards. A strong foundation is also important for friendships. We are going to create a picture stand to help you remember four things you can do to have and be a great friend."

Ask youth to write on each card one of the following words using large letters (on the unlined side). As you discuss each of the following words, encourage teens to write phrases or other words (in smaller letters) that explain or describe the key word. (Adapt the following dialogue to fit your comfort level in discussion, or read the descriptions in the student journal).

G – God: Make God a part of your relationships. That doesn't mean that all of your friends must be Christians, but it does mean that the love of God should be noticeable in your actions and words.

R – Risk: If we don't take risks, we won't grow. When we took our first steps as babies, we risked falling. Likewise, there are many risks worth taking in our friendships: sharing secrets, giving compliments, trying new ideas together, being willing to work through problems, and so on.

O – Openness: The best friendships occur when both persons are truly open with each other, and that openness is respected by honoring confidentiality and trustworthiness.

W – Worth: What difference would it make in our relationships if we treated our friends as if they were worth more than anything else in the world? What if we saw our friends as God sees them—persons of incredible worth and value because of who they are rather than what they do or how they look?

Once all four cards are complete, use clear tape to connect them in a square shape, words facing out. Notch the frames on two opposite sides, forming a picture stand. Or, tape a picture in the middle so that the cards become a picture frame.

OR

E-Friendship (5–7 minutes)

One of the most popular items teens send to one another by e-mail are messages about the nature of friendship. These poems, drawings, quotations, or thoughts about friendship usually encourage recipients to forward the item to ten friends, including the one who originally sent the message. If enough youth in your class have access to e-mail, consider doing this activity. The messages will remind them of the session topic throughout the week.

Ask:
• Have you ever received an e-mail message that talked about the qualities of a true friend?
• What kinds of statements, poems, or quotations were included in the e-mail?
• When you receive those messages, do you forward them to your friends?

An alternative approach for this activity is to ask participants to write their answers in their student journals.

Provide small pieces of paper and pens or pencils.

Remember to e-mail group members with a listing of e-mail addresses.

Provide student journals and pens or pencils. Plan to play soft, meditative background music.

Go With God

Provide at least two leaves for each group member and markers.

On the tree created last week, mark a branch with the word "Friends."

This activity will be an ending option each week. If you chose to do it the first week, plan to use it at the end of each session. It is not too late to begin the activity this week.

Say: "Let's compose our own friendship e-mail and forward it to others. Who knows how far our message might reach? Think about what we might say that would reflect what we have learned today about friendship."

Ask: "What could we as Christians say about friendship that might be different from what you've read in other e-mails you have received?" (Take two or three minutes to begin generating ideas.)

Distribute pens and small pieces of paper. Say: "Write down your email address, if you have one, on the piece of paper. I will send everyone a message listing class members' e-mail addresses. As you think of ideas for our group e-mail message, send them to other group members and ask for feedback. You may also compose a rough draft and forward to other group members for comment. We will work on this activity for a week or so until we create something exciting and meaningful."

 ## QTJ—Quiet Time Journaling (7–9 minutes)

Distribute student journals and pens. Say: "It's time to reflect on our session topic by journaling. Remember, your journals are safely put away after each session. They are for "your eyes only." Journaling is not about creative sentences, correct spelling, or answers. The idea is to reflect on ways you can be a great friend."

Allow youth about five minutes to write in their journals. Remind students to complete the "This Week's Challenge." Check again to see that class members have written their names on their journals before collecting.

Rooted and Grounded in Love (3–4 minutes)

Distribute at least two leaves to each student. Also distribute markers. Say: "Each week we will be adding to our tree as a visual reminder of ways we can grow more like Jesus in our relationships. On one leaf, write some idea or truth you've learned today. On the other write a principle or attitude you think is important to remember about good relationships with friends. (Youth can make additional leaves.) As you attach your leaves to the "Friends" branch, silently pray that God will help you to be a great friend to others as well as fill your life with great friendships."

AND/OR

Connected

To close, ask youth to form a circle, crossing their right arms over their left and holding hands. Say: "The way we are connected reminds us that we are a community of friends, a group that always offers love and acceptance. When we leave, we will turn outward and flip our arms over our heads, symbolizing that we can take Christ's love into the world." End with a short prayer or your group's traditional blessing.

Someone to Help

Topic: Finding Adult Friends and Mentors

Scripture: Proverbs 9:9; 12:15; 15:22; 18:4; 19:20; 24:5-6; 25:11; 29:1

Key Verse: Listen to advice and accept instruction, that you may gain wisdom for the future. (Proverbs 19:20)

Take Home—Learning: Youth will understand how to choose and work with a mentor, and they will begin to think about someone they could ask to be their mentor.

Younger Youth and This Topic

Younger teens need and want adult role models. Contrary to what many people think, parents are still the most important shapers of values in teens' lives. Teens seek out peer groups that match their values, values that originated with their parents. Early adolescents are greatly influenced by their peer group when it comes to visible and tangible items such as clothing styles, music preferences, diets, language, and their rooms. But when it comes to life's deeper questions, teens genuinely appreciate the help of mentors. In fact, they often prefer adults other than their parents until they have sufficiently separated from them in their late teen years.

Mentors are like supporting actors—they help youth shine in the spotlight. The best mentors don't provide an abundance of answers, but they help youth to clarify their questions. Mentors are most helpful to teens during times when they

- are asking deep, sincere questions about people/situations that require thoughtful feedback;
- are having a tough time making a difficult decision;
- are torn between doing what they want to do and what they know is the right thing to do.

A good mentor doesn't see his or her role as telling youth what to believe. Teenagers' convictions frequently are undergoing rapid development and change, so good mentors help youth to embrace the issues of the day as opportunities to shed clarity on the questions of life.

Help your youth to think about their relationships with adults and the roles those adults play—teachers, coaches, friends, leaders, and parents. The concept of faith mentor may be completely new to the students; it is your job to help them understand the role a faith mentor can play in their lives. Follow-up is crucial. If your church does not already have a mentoring program in place, talk with the pastor or youth director about their support in implementing such a program.

Search Institute has identified forty assets that youth need. Number three is "other adult relationships," which is defined as "Young person receives support from three or more nonparent adults."
—Search Institute

From The Assets Approach: *Giving Kids What They Need to Succeed.* © 1997 by Search Institute.

Theology and the Topic

Younger teens are developing the ability to think through profound issues and complicated moral dilemmas, but they lack the worldview and wealth of experience that adults offer. Probing life's deep issues signifies a new dimension in a teen's spirituality—one reason why mentors are crucial during this period of adolescence. The questions that arise from self-doubt or a search for truth can lead to deep spiritual growth if teens are guided to develop a personal theology rather than a religion of rules.

In an age when the family may or may not help youth develop their Christian faith, it becomes even more important that the church commit to helping each teen find an adult faith mentor. If, indeed, faith is "caught" more than "taught," we must invest a great deal of our youth-ministry time and energy in efforts to connect youth and adults. Christian faith is not a solo endeavor. We all need a community of believers to challenge us, to disciple us, and to love us along our journey.

You and the Scripture

Take a few minutes to browse **The Book of Proverbs**, especially **Chapters 10–15**.

• Early to bed, early to rise . . .
• God helps those . . .
• The Lord giveth . . .

Perhaps you learned these proverbs as a child—bad theology and all. Are there other proverbs or quotations you live by, consciously or unconsciously?

The Bible proverbs that mean the most to us are generally those in which we can see ourselves. As our experience with people, money, and knowledge grows, our ability to identify ourselves in various proverbs also grows. Take a few minutes to browse the Book of Proverbs, especially Chapters 10–15. Which proverbs seem particularly true for you?

Now consider some of these proverbs while thinking of your youth. Which proverbs would be difficult for them to understand due to their lack of experience or lesser ability to think abstractly?

The Book of Proverbs includes passages spoken, written, and edited by various sages, the most famous probably being King Solomon. The theology of these writers was rooted in an understanding of God acquired through keen observation of creation and human behavior. As a result, the Book of Proverbs exalts intellectual study and wisdom more than personal experience as the way to know God.

• To what extent is your faith rooted in intellectual study, in thinking, and in logic?

• How can you encourage youth whose understanding of God is rooted more in experience and story to develop a love for proverbs?

Someone to Help

Scripture: Proverbs 9:9; 12:15; 15:22; 18:4; 19:20; 24:5-6; 25:11; 29:1

Take Home—Learning: Youth will understand how to choose and work with a mentor, and they will begin to think about someone they could ask to be their mentor.

 indicates key activity. If time is limited, focus here.

activity	time	preparation	supplies
get ready			
Are You a Wise One?	7–9 minutes	Prepare proverbs index cards (with underlined answers) to read aloud.	index cards, pens, small prizes (optional)
jump in			
Proverbs in Pieces	6–8 minutes	Duplicate Proverbs in Pieces handout (page 50), then cut apart the pieces as indicated.	scissors, tape, handouts
Circles of Connection	4–6 minutes	Prepare a personal Circles of Connection diagram. Prepare a chart listing categories in the margin on page 23.	student journals, pens, large sheet of paper, marker
look for life			
Practice Asking	4–6 minutes	Duplicate Will You Be My Mentor? handout (page 51).	handouts
QTJ—Quiet Time Journaling	7–9 minutes	Obtain soft, meditative music to play while students are journaling.	soft background music tape or CD
go with god			
Rooted and Grounded in Love and/or Huddle Prayer	3–4 minutes	Prepare two leaves per person. Write the word, "Mentors" on a tree branch. Invite parents to attend.	two green leaves per person, markers, tape

Get Ready

Provide three index cards per person, pens or pencils, and small prizes (optional).

On one each of three index cards, write the proverbs listed in the activity. Underline the portion in parentheses. When reading aloud the proverbs, do not read underlined endings.

Source of proverbs: http://cogweb.english. ucsb.edu/Discourse/ Proverbs/Miscellaneous .html

Jump In

Provide Proverbs in Pieces handout (page 50) and tape.

Duplicate Proverbs in Pieces handout to 11-by-17 paper, if possible. Cut each proverb into three pieces according to the lines. Shuffle before distributing to participants.

Are You a Wise One? (7–9 minutes)

Give students three index cards apiece, and instruct them to write their names at the top of each of the cards. Say: "I'm going to read aloud the beginnings of several proverbs. On a separate card, write your best guess as to how each proverb ends. I will collect all the cards for each proverb before moving to the next one."

One at a time, read aloud the following partial proverbs, pausing to allow youth to write their endings to each one. Collect their answer cards after each proverb, and shuffle their cards along with the question/answer card you read aloud.

Proverb 1: There's a Nigerian proverb: "He who is being carried . . . "
   (does not realize how far the town is.)
Proverb 2: There's a Yiddish proverb: "If you sit in a hot bath . . . "
   (you think the whole town is warm.)
Proverb 3: There's a Libyan proverb: "Instruction in youth . . . "
   (is like engraving in stone.)

Now say: "I'm going to read aloud your endings to the first proverb, as well as the correct ending. Choose the ending you think is correct. We will vote after I've read all the proverb endings."

Read aloud the first proverb in its entirety. Then read aloud each proposed ending as well as the correct one. Ask each participant to vote for the one he or she thinks is correct. After everyone has voted, reveal the correct ending. Give one point to anyone who chose the correct ending. Also give one point for every vote a person received for her or his proverb ending. Continue this process with the second and third proverbs. Award a small prize, such as a small book of proverbs or an inexpensive dictionary, to the winner(s).

If time permits, ask, What do you think these proverbs mean? (The student's interpretations may be different from yours.)

Proverbs in Pieces (6–8 minutes)

Ask:
• Why do you think proverbs are common in many of the world's countries? *(They are easy to remember; they say something wise in a few words; they are sometimes humorous; and so on.)*
• Have you memorized any of your favorite proverbs?

Say: Thousands of years ago, King Solomon was considered to be the wisest person in the world. He probably wrote many of the Proverbs in the Bible. We're going to use a little of our wisdom to reconstruct some of them. I'm going to distribute portions of the Proverbs to each of you. If you receive a piece that lists the chapter and verse, then you have received part one of the Proverb.

Divide and distribute the Proverbs in Pieces among the participants. (In a small class, each youth may receive more than one piece.) Ask a student

Good friends

who received one of the first segments to read aloud his or her proverb, then ask the other youth to check for a matching completion. Tape the completed proverbs on a focal wall, rearranging segments as necessary. Work together until all the proverbs are completed, then read them again in their entirety.

Ask:
• Did you have difficulty understanding any of the proverbs?
• Did you detect a common theme among the proverbs?
• Were there similar messages in the proverbs?

Say: "These proverbs deal with listening to the advice and instruction of others who are wiser. Many different people offer us advice and instruction. Coaches train us in a skill, and teachers help us to understand and learn information. There's another wise person who helps us to ask probing questions and to find the answers ourselves. We refer to such persons as mentors.

Ask:
• Have any of you ever had a mentor?
• (If yes) How did that person help you?
• (If no) What are some reasons people choose and work with a mentor?

 Circles of Connection (4–6 minutes)

Distribute student journals and pens or pencils.

Say: "We've discussed some reasons to consider working with a mentor. Now we're going to think about some of the people you might choose to be your mentor. Turn to page 12 in your student journal. In the "Circles of Connection" activity, there is a small circle in the center. That circle represents you. In the other circles, write the names of adults (other than your parents) whom you know well. The closer the name is to the center circle, the closer your relationship should be to that person. Think about the adults you know, but especially focus on those who already influence your life in some way. For example, here is what my diagram would have looked like at your age." *(Briefly describe your diagram.)*

Allow youth several minutes to work on this activity, then say: "Once you have finished naming adults, circle ones who could be your mentor in terms of your school work, your faith, your friendships, your hobbies or interests, and appealing careers. List possible categories for each potential mentor.

Wait a few minutes for youth to complete this portion of the activity. Be alert to any students who have trouble identifying adults in their lives as possible mentors.

Ask: "Which category was the most difficult for you to think of someone who could be a mentor? How do you feel about asking one or more of these people to be your mentor?"

Provide student journals, pens or pencils, a large sheet of paper, and markers.

Before the session, write these categories on a large sheet of paper: Schoolwork; Faith; Friendships; Hobbies and Interests; Careers. Also, using the instructions in the activity, prepare a diagram showing what your own relationships to adults looked like when you were a teen.

Someone to Help

Look for Life

Provide Will You Be My Mentor? handout (page 51).

Duplicate as many copies of the handout as you expect participants.

Provide student journals and pens.

Go With God

Provide two tree leaves per person, markers, and tape.

Add the word "Mentors" to another tree branch.

If possible, invite a group of parents and other adults to join youth at the end of this session.

This activity will be an ending option each week. If you chose to do it the first week, plan to use it at the end of each session.

 ## Practice Asking (4–6 minutes)

Teenagers often feel uncomfortable approaching a potential mentor to ask for her or his help. Include time for youth to practice asking adults to be their mentors.

Say: "Sometimes deciding what to say or how to go about asking a potential mentor can be intimidating. We're going to practice that skill." Distribute the Will You Be My Mentor? handout. "This handout provides several tips for asking someone to be a mentor. Right now, choose a partner, and using the sample script, roleplay how you might ask someone to be your mentor."

 ## QTJ—Quiet Time Journaling (7–9 minutes)

Distribute the student journals and pens. Say: "This is the time each week when you have opportunity to reflect on the session topic by journaling. Remember, each week I place the journals in a safe place. No one sees your journal but you. Don't worry about using correct grammar or spelling. The purpose of this journaling is to give you time to consider and identify ways you can be a great friend. Be sure to answer the questions on page 13."

Students may either work in their seats or move to a private corner to write.

Rooted and Grounded in Love (3–4 minutes)

Distribute two tree leaves and a marker to each person. Then say: "Each week we've been adding leaves to our tree as a visual reminder of ways we can grow more like Jesus in our relationships. On one or both of your leaves, write a fact or truth you've learned today or a proverb you think is important to remember about good relationships with mentors. Tape the leaves to the "Mentors" branch of the tree. As you attach the leaves, pray silently that God will lead you to some great mentors."

AND/OR

Huddle Prayer

If you have parents and other adults joining the session now, direct teens to huddle while the adults circle around them. Ask adults to place their hands on the shoulders of the youth and to close in a prayer for them (both those who are present and those who are absent.)

On the Team

Topic: Cooperating With and Respecting Others: Teamwork

Scripture: Romans 12:9-21; Philippians 2:1-4

Key Verse: Let each of you look not to your own interests, but to the interests of others. (Philippians 2:4)

Take—Home Learning: God has created us to be in community with one another.

Younger Youth and This Topic

Most teens are capable of cooperating and working with their peers. Their instinct as younger youth is to band together, and their desire to belong usually causes them to be sensitive to the best interests of the group or team. But what teens often lack is a desire to cooperate with everyone—store clerks, other adults at church, teachers, parents, and so on. Early adolescents haven't yet completely grasped how much our society is based on cooperation. You can help them broaden their understanding and support for what is good for the larger group.

Respect is a more difficult concept for younger youth to comprehend. They believe respect should be earned, and, certainly, this is a valid point. However, we respect some people simply because of their age, their viewpoint, or their level of authority. The fifth commandment doesn't say, Honor your father and mother if they have earned your respect!

Here are some points to emphasize with the youth:

- Cooperation is in their own best interest. Nobody enjoys working or being with uncooperative people.
- Their friends appreciate and need their cooperation on group projects.
- Life is easier and a lot more fun when we work as a team.
- Respect is not the same as blindly accepting someone's flaws.
- Another word that is defined much the same as respect is *value*. When we respect someone, we show that we value him or her as a person.
- People don't have to be perfect to be worthy of our respect.

On the Team

Leaders Guide

Theology and the Topic

Few images in Paul's letters are as memorable as his description of Jesus' followers. He refers to us as the body of Christ, made up of many members—each with its own function contributing to the whole. What a perfect image for younger youth to hear and embrace. Knowing that they are part of a beautiful body not only boosts their self-image, but also strengthens their self-concept as they recognize that they are gifted by God with skills, abilities, talents, and gifts useful to the church and to the world. We were not created to be individuals on our own; instead, we were created to be in community with one another.

As our globe "shrinks" with instant media coverage, the awareness of our interdependence grows. Events in one area of the world affect the economy, people, even the climate in another, seemingly far distant area. Unity is not something we create; it already exists whether we recognize it or not. Thanks to science classes, youth are already aware of the interrelatedness of all life in creation. It is the responsibility of the church to help them embrace the truths that God is the one who creates life to be connected and that life is more fulfilling when we live connected to God and in community with one another.

You and the Scripture

Romans, Chapter 12 begins the second section of Paul's letter: one that focuses on moral, ethical, and behavioral instructions. This particular passage draws inspiration from the wisdom tradition of books like the Proverbs. Here are a few other points to note about the passage:

- 12:9—"Hate what is evil, hold fast to what is good." This is one of the few Scripture verses that instructs us to hate. In context, *hate* is the opposite of *hold fast*. In this instance, love is *agape* love, a self-giving action for others made possible because of the Spirit of God.
- 12:10—"Love one another with mutual affection." In this phrase, *love* is a different Greek word: *philadelphia*. Its meaning is familial affection or brotherly love.
- 12:14—"Bless those who persecute you." Only occasionally does Paul make a reference to the teachings of Jesus. This verse may be one of them. (See Luke 6:28.)
- 12:16—"Do not be haughty, but associate with the lowly." Associating with the lowly is not a phrase meaning simply to socialize with them. This verse can also be translated, "give yourselves to humble tasks."
- 12:17—"Do not repay anyone evil for evil." This common Christian teaching (also found in 1 Thessalonians 5:15 and 1 Peter 3:9) reminds us that we aren't called to do only what the majority feels is good or right. Ours is a higher calling: to do what is inherently good and noble in everyone's eyes.

- Which of the instructions in this passage are hardest for you to carry out?
- What are three things you can do this week to live out these instructions?

Spend a few minutes reading the passage **Romans 12:9-21** before continuing.

Since the last session, have you felt more like you have overcome evil with good or more like you have overcome good with evil? From where did you receive your strength to do good?

On the Team

Scripture: Romans 12:9-21; Philippians 2:1-4

Take-Home Learning: God has created us to be in community with one another.

 indicates key activity. If time is limited, focus here.

activity	time	preparation	supplies
get ready			
A Team Creation	7–12 minutes	Prepare paint prior to the session. Place damp towels in plastic bags. Collect old shirts.	finger paint, newspaper, containers, damp towels, old shirts, tape
jump in			
I'm Lichen It!"	6–9 minutes	Survey the church property or a park for samples of lichen.	samples of lichen
look for life			
Instructions for the Team	8–15 minutes	Duplicate Instructions for the Team handout (page 52). Cut apart and place inside tennis-ball can.	tennis ball, can, handouts
QTJ—Quiet Time Journaling	5–6 minutes	Obtain soft background music to play during journaling.	soft meditative music tape, student journals, pens or pencils
go with god			
Rooted and Grounded in Love	3–4 minutes	Prepare two leaves per person. Write on one of the tree branches the words "Teamwork and Cooperation."	two leaves per person, markers, tape
O, What a Gifted Web We Weave	4–8 minutes	Review the activity instructions on page 30.	large ball of yarn

Get Ready

Provide plastic paper or newspaper, large pieces of paper, variety of fingerpaints, old shirts, damp towels, and tape.

Cover tables with plastic or newspaper, then spread large pieces of paper. (If you have several tables, place them together.) Provide several containers of fingerpaint in a variety of colors and old shirts to cover youths' clothing. Have damp towels on hand for spills.

Jump In

Before the session, check trees, large rocks, or fence posts around the church to see if you can locate lichen (usually a thin, greenish-grey growth). If you aren't able to find any lichen on your church property, look in a local park to find a branch or rock with lichen. Take it to the session.

Note: Some scholars believe the manna eaten by the Israelites when they were wandering in the desert was a type of lichen that was easily scattered by the wind.

 A Team Creation (7–12 minutes)

As the youth arrive, direct them to the tables prepared with fingerpaints and paper. Say: "Use the fingerpaints to create a scene that represents teamwork and cooperation. As a group you may choose what to paint, but everyone must work together in silence." Point out the old shirts and damp cloths.

After approximately four minutes to work on the painting, encourage youth to quickly clean up the paint supplies and wash their hands.

When youth reassemble, enlist their help in hanging the painting on the wall. Then ask and discuss the following questions:

- What do you see in this painting?
- What was it like working together in silence?
- Was it difficult to decide what your contribution to the overall painting would be?
- In what ways did you find it necessary to cooperate with others?

I'm Lichen It! (6–9 minutes)

If you found lichen on the church property, take class members outside to show them the tree or rock. (If you brought in a sample of lichen, display it for youth at this time.) Ask: "Does anyone know what this growth is called?" (If one or more youth answer yes, ask what and how they know about lichen.)

If possible, continue the discussion outside and say: "Lichen is actually two separate organisms combined—a fungus and a photosynthetic algae. Each one depends on the other for its survival. Do you know the name for two organisms that survive in this fashion? (*symbiosis*) The fungus and the algae combine to form a completely new organism that receives nourishment from air, rainwater, and light. Over time, lichen can even transform a rock into soil by gradually breaking down the rock with a self-produced acid. Did you know that lichen is the primary vegetation in Iceland and Greenland?"

Ask: "In what ways are people similar to lichen?" (*Our survival depends on others; together we can do more than we can alone, and so on.*)

Ask: "Have you ever considered that our relationship with God is also a symbiotic one." Allow time for comments, and then ask:

- In what ways do we rely on God?
- In what ways does God rely on us?

Return to the classroom before beginning the next activity.

Instructions for the Team (8–15 minutes)

Ask:
• How many of you have ever played or served on a team?
• What methods did the coach use to teach you the necessary rules or skills?

Say: "Our Scriptures today resemble a coach's instructions to a team. Paul was instructing the Christians in Rome about how to live in a Christian community. But, just as a coach's instructions given in practice often have to be adapted during the game, the instructions in God's Word must be applied to our real-life situations. That's what we're going to try to do using this activity."

Call attention to the tennis ball and can of verses. Say: "Inside this can are Scripture verses from Romans 12 and Philippians 2. I will draw a verse from the can and read it aloud before tossing this ball to one of you. Whoever catches the ball must think quickly and explain how the verse relates to living in community with one another.

"For example, you might explain how practicing the verse would help others or why you believe it's important for Christians to act in the way the verse teaches. Your answer doesn't have to be long or complicated. When each person finishes, he or she will choose someone else, throw the ball, and repeat the process."

Make sure everyone understands the instructions and receives a turn to catch the ball and react to a verse before going around a second time.

 QTJ—Quiet Time Journaling (5–6 minutes)

Distribute Bibles, student journals, and pens. Say: "Just as we've done each week, now is your opportunity to focus on our topic by using a journal. Your journals have been in a safe place since last week. No one sees what you've written except you. Use this time to think about ways you can try to interact lovingly with your friends, family, and people you encounter each day." Students may work in their seats or move to a quiet corner of the room.

Play soft background music for about five minutes while teens write in their journals. Remind them to complete "This Week's Challenge" in their student journals. Check journals for names before collecting them at the end of the session.

Rooted and Grounded in Love (3–4 minutes)

Distribute two leaves and a marker to each person. Say: "Each week we've been adding to our tree as a visual reminder of ways we can grow more like Jesus in our relationships. On one or more leaves, write a fact or truth that you've learned today or a Scripture verse you think is important to remember about being a team member and cooperating with others. Tape the leaves to

Provide a tennis ball (or a similar size ball), tennis-ball can (or use another container), Instructions for Team Scripture Verses handout (page 52).

Duplicate the Instructions for Team Scripture Verses handout (page 52), cut apart the Scripture verses, and place inside the can or container.

Provide Bibles, student journals, pens, and soft background music.

Go With God

Provide two tree leaves and a marker per person and tape.

Mark a tree branch with the words "Teamwork and Cooperation."

L e a d e r ' s   G u i d e

On the Team

the "Teamwork and Cooperation" branch of the tree. As you attach the leaves, pray silently that God will help you this week to look to the interests of others as you relate to them in various ways."

OR

O, What a Gifted Web We Weave (4–8 minutes)

Provide a ball of yarn.

Direct the entire group to stand in a circle. Hold on to the loose end of the yarn with one hand, and hold the ball with the other.

Say: "One important responsibility of a coach is to encourage his/her team members. Without encouragement it is difficult to remain motivated and confident in your abilities. As Christian team members, we need to encourage one another, too. As an example, we are going to play another game. This time we're going to toss around a ball of yarn. First, I will hold the end of the string and toss the ball to one of you. Whoever catches the ball, hold on to the string and toss the ball to another person across the circle. But before tossing, name one or more skills, gifts, or talents you think that person contributes to make him or her an important part of the group. I will go first."

Hold the end of the yarn, then model how you'd like the youth to encourage one another. Choose a youth, affirm him or her, then toss the ball of yarn. After everyone has tossed the ball, and a web has been formed with the yarn, ask the following questions:

• What have we created with our yarn?
• How is a web a good metaphor for the Christian life?

Say: "We are connected to one another and to God in ways we can see but also in ways we rarely even think about. Let's close by silently thanking God for all the connections we share.

Good Friends

Eye to Eye

Topic: Conflict Resolution and Forgiveness

Scripture: Ephesians 4:1-32; James 3:2-12

Key Verse: With all humility and gentleness, with patience, bearing with one another in love (Ephesians 4:2)

Take—Home Learning: Knowing how to deal with conflicts is one of the most important skills for teenagers to learn; it will help them in all areas of their current and future lives.

Younger Youth and This Topic

Conflict is common in the lives of younger youth. Whether it's disagreements about family rules, petty bickering among siblings, or backlash from the rumor mill among friends at school, youth experience various kinds of conflicts almost daily. Conflict is common, especially within the family, because teens are seeking more control over their own lives. The problem is that while youth quickly become adept at whining, gossiping, shouting, bullying, or whatever else it takes to get their way, they don't always learn the skills needed to handle conflict resolution successfully and peacefully.

Younger youth often possess a strong fear of isolation. When conflict erupts between friends, each person immediately wants to know which side his or her friends will choose. If friends do take take sides, the relationship quickly becomes polarized, potentially ending the friendship. When a family conflict flares, young teens quickly share their plights with their friends in an effort to bolster support and their sense of "right-ness" in the situation.

Still, conflict can be a positive thing if dealt with appropriately. Disagreements between friends or family members can be opportunities for teenagers to try to view situations from another person's perspective. If conflicts are aired and then resolved in supportive, respectful, and mutually beneficial ways, teens learn new cognitive skills and grow in the ability to think independently yet not egotistically. In this session, you will help youth to discover a simple process for stepping back from conflicts and stepping up to win-win solutions.

Theology and the Topic

If we were to list the top three themes in Scripture, conflict would surely be one of the three. Since the attacks on the World Trade Towers and the

Pentagon on September 11, 2001, conflict is often on the minds of most Christians. In particular, the response to this tragedy/conflict has helped us to rediscover how connected we are to one another as children of God and how much we need to connect with God.

Though conflicts occur for many reasons, disconnection with others is a common thread. The ways we choose to resolve conflict reveals much about our desire to reconnect with one another. Usually, conflict resolution requires a conversion of the heart, a greater trust in others, and a deeper faithfulness to God. Through our efforts, we can eventually look back and see the ways God is at work in us through conflict.

The differences we observe between people are part of life's diversity, and are, therefore, good as well as normal. The tension created by our differences is not automatically negative since it provides an opportunity for growth through the conflict. Seeking an end to all conflict is an unrealistic endeavor; instead, we must strive for the presence of *shalom*—a just peace—in the world. This peace is possible only through the love of God that empowers us to forgive, to reconcile with one another, and then to experience healing.

You and the Scripture

Read Ephesians 4:1-3, James 3:2-12, and Matthew 5:9.

What are some causes of conflict, as well as some actions to prevent conflict that are implied or stated in the Scripture passage?

• Causes of conflict

• Actions to prevent conflict

How does the passage in the Book of James help you to answer these questions:

• What do our words have to do with the conflicts we encounter?
• When do your words most often cause you trouble?
• How is God calling you to be a peacemaker through your words and actions?

Scan the listings for current, prime-time television programs as well as ads for current movies to see how many of these shows and movies focus on violent conflict. In light of Matthew 5:9, how can you answer these questions:

• Why do you think violence is a common theme on television and in movies?
• Which television programs do you regularly watch, and why?
• What change of habits does peacemaking require of us?

Good Friends

Eye to Eye

Scripture: Proverbs 20:3; Ephesians 4:1-4, 22-32; James 3:2-12

Take–Home Learning: Knowing how to deal with conflicts is one of the most important skills for teenagers to learn; it will help them in all areas of their current and future lives.

 indicates key activity. If time is limited, focus here.

activity	time	preparation	supplies
get ready			
Stomp It	4–6 minutes	Cut as many pieces of yarn (20 inches long) as you expect youth. Blow up the same number of balloons.	yarn, small balloons
jump in			
Bitter or Better? Scenarios	10–14 minutes	Prepare as many sets of cards as you expect students. Duplicate scenarios (page 53).	two index cards (two colors) per person, scenarios
look for life			
Conflict: Hot and Cold	7–9 minutes	Review the activity in the student journal (page 20).	extra Bibles, student journals, pens
Three T's—Times Two	7–10 minutes	Copy and cut apart Bitter or Better? Scenarios (page 53). Follow instructions in the margin on page 35.	large sheets of paper, markers, scenarios
QTJ—Quiet Time Journaling	6–8 minutes	Obtain soft background music to play during journaling.	meditative music tape/CD, student journals, pens or pencils
go with god			
Rooted and Grounded in Love or 70 x 7!	3–4 minutes	Prepare two leaves per person. Write on one branch the words "Resolving Conflicts." Decide on closing prayer.	two leaves per person, markers, tape

Eye to Eye

Get Ready

Provide balloons and yarn.

Before the session, blow up as many balloons as you expect participants. Also cut the same number of foot-long pieces of yarn.

Jump In

Provide index cards (if possible, two different colors per participant), Bitter or Better? Scenarios handout (page 53).

If possible, use two different color index cards, or write the word *Bitter* on one set of cards and the word *Better* on the second set of cards. Review the scenarios from the handout, or if you have the time during the week, collect real-life scenarios that describe a recent conflict with a youth's family member or a friend.

Stomp It (4–6 minutes)

Play the popular "balloon stomp" party game. Using the yarn strings, tie balloons around the ankles of each youth. When you yell "Go," everyone tries to step on and pop the balloons tied to others while also protecting his or her own balloon. The last person with an inflated balloon wins. Play as many rounds as time allows.

Ask:
- How does a conflicting situation between two people compare to our stomping another person's balloon? (*In conflicts, we usually try to protect our own point of view while squashing the other person's point of view.*)
- Why do people in conflict with one another usually try to get their own way in the situation? (*One reason is that we think we know what is best for us.*)

 ## Bitter or Better? Scenarios (10–14 minutes)

Say: "Let's play a game called Bitter or Better. The object of the game is to provide answers to lifelike scenarios that demonstrate you are growing better and not bitter in conflict resolution."

Ask for three participants to play the game. If more than three youth volunteer, draw names to see who will play first. Direct the three youth to sit at the front of the room in chairs facing everyone else. Give each remaining class member two index cards that are two different colors (or the Bitter/Better cards).

Say: "I'm going to read aloud a short scenario demonstrating a conflict you might face in your life. The three contestants will have ten seconds to think about their responses before telling us what they would do in those particular situations. Those of you who are not playing the game each have two cards. One (*first color card*) represents an answer you believe would cause that person or relationship to grow bitter. The second card (*color of second card*) represents an answer you think would cause that person or relationship to grow better. After each contestant gives his or her answer, I'll ask the rest of the group to vote."

Continue: "Next, I need a scorekeeper. (Choose a volunteer.) The contestants will receive five points for every "Better" card and will lose five points for every "Bitter" card. I'll begin with the player on the left. We will play three rounds, and each round will begin with a different player. Are there any questions?"

While playing the game, only one person will give an answer to each scenario. Encourage persons to defend their "bitter or better" votes—especially if their votes are in the minority. Encourage discussion.

Conflict: Hot and Cold (7–9 minutes)

Say: "One of the most important skills you can learn in life is how to deal with conflict, because at some point in life, people experience conflict in friendships, family, work, and marriage. Even Jesus encountered conflict with the religious leaders of his day about his teachings and beliefs, but he chose to deal with the conflict in ways that prevented bitterness. It's not whether you experience conflict but how you choose to deal with it that is most important. Let's look closer at some reasons for conflict and ways we can respond."

Form three groups. Assign each group one of the following Scripture passages: Ephesians 4:1-4 and Proverbs 20:3; Ephesians 4:22-32; James 3:2-12. Distribute the student journals and instruct groups to turn to "Conflict: Hot and Cold" (page 20). Direct students to complete this section using the Scriptures. Allow three or four minutes for groups to work on their assignments.

Say: "Choose two group members—one to report the group's findings and another to read aloud the Scripture verse that you think is the most important." Wait a moment for groups to decide, then begin small-group reports. Note any duplicate or similar group responses.

OR

 ## Three T's—Times Two (7–10 minutes)

Say: "There are three common ways of dealing with conflict. Often, our first instinct is to 'take it out' (like a skunk), which means we take out our anger and frustration on the other person. What are some of the ways we 'take it out' on others?" (*verbal assaults, physical violence, slamming doors, and so on*) List responses on the chart you prepared earlier. Then ask, "What usually happens in a conflict when we take this approach?"

Say: "Another common response is to 'tuck it in' (like a turtle), which means we bury our response to the conflict. Sometimes we try to avoid a confrontation by running away from the situation or attempting to ignore it, even if it eats us up inside. Can you think of examples of people taking the 'tuck it in' approach?" (List responses on chart.) Ask, "Is this way of dealing with conflict healthy or unhealthy?"

Say: "A third way to deal with conflict is to 'talk it out.' The goal in this approach is to find a common ground and a solution that is acceptable to all involved."

Continue: "Now, let's look at some ways to 'talk it out' in a conflict situation. The first step is to **try** to see the other person's point of view. This may require stepping away from the conflict for a while. Or, it may mean that you ask the person a question: 'Can you help me understand why you think that way?' The second step is to **think.** Ask yourself questions like*: What would Jesus do in this situation? How can I be a peacemaker? How can I choose the way of love?* The third step is to talk it out **together** and to listen carefully.

Eye to Eye

Provide student journals, pens or pencils.

Provide large sheets of paper and markers.

On a large sheet of paper, write in columns the three ways of dealing with conflict: take it out, tuck it in, and talk it out. Leave room for writing around the three methods.

On another large sheet of paper, write the three T's: Try, Think, Together.

Acting as a peacemaker could mean giving up what you want for the sake of the relationship. Other times you might discover a completely new solution."

Provide Bitter or Better? Scenarios handout (page 53).

Say: "We're going to review the 'Bitter or Better?' Scenarios we discussed previously." Keeping the same small groups, give each group two scenarios. Instruct each group to re-read the scenario before discussing what would likely happen if the person involved attempted each of the three ways of dealing with conflict as well as what might occur during each of the "Try-Think-Together" steps. Call time after one or two minutes, then instruct groups to discuss the second portion of the assignment. No reporting back is necessary.

QTJ—Quiet Time Journaling (6–8 minutes)

Provide student journals, extra sheets of paper, and pens or pencils.

Distribute Bibles, student journals, writing paper, and pens. Direct the students to pages 20–23 in the journal to follow the instructions there. If you did not use the Three T's activity earlier, you may need to introduce the question, How does a skunk deal with conflict? What about a turtle? And talk a bit about the repercussions (good and bad) of both types of responses before students begin to write.

God With God

Rooted and Grounded in Love (3–4 minutes)

Provide two tree leaves and one marker per person and tape.

Attach the words "Resolving Conflicts" to one of the tree branches.

Distribute two leaves and a marker to each person. Say: "Each week we've been adding to our tree as a visual reminder of ways we can grow more like Jesus in our relationships. On one or both leaves, write a fact or truth that you've learned today or principle or Scripture you think is important to remember about resolving conflicts. Tape the leaves to the 'Resolving Conflicts' branch of the tree. As you attach the leaves, pray silently that God will guide you as you attempt to be a peacemaker in the world."

AND/OR

70 x 7!

Ask teens to form a circle, then read aloud Matthew 18:21-22. Say: "After a conflict, it's important to forgive the other person. Peacemakers do not hold grudges. When Jesus said we should forgive someone "seventy times seven," he meant that we should continue to be forgiving."

Ask teens to hold hands and conclude the session with the circle prayer of your choice (the Lord's Prayer, a popcorn prayer, a silent prayer, and so forth).

We're JUST Friends

Topic: Friendships with the Opposite Sex

Scripture: Romans 12:9-21

Key Verse: Love one another with mutual affection; outdo one another in showing honor. (Romans 12:10)

Take—Home Learning: Friendships with members of the opposite sex are appropriate and don't have to lead to dating. Through these relationships we learn how to understand and treat others.

Younger Youth and This Topic

Recall your own days as a young teen. Do you remember how important it was to be liked? Can you remember the things you did to be popular—or at least well-liked—by other students? When did you start socializing with members of the opposite sex?

Psychologists tell us that one of the interpersonal needs during middle adolescent years is a friendship with someone of the opposite sex. In fact, younger youth typically are moving from having only same-sex friends to having multiple friends of the opposite sex and a preference for mixed-gender groups. Girls appreciate friendships with guys because guys tend to be less emotional and can keep things in perspective. Guys often seek friendships with girls because girls are can more easily participate in serious conversations and openly express their emotions without feeling the need to protect a macho male persona. A more basic reason is that members of both sexes simply enjoy hanging out with someone different than themselves.

At the same time, opposite-sex relationships can be stressful due to several factors. First, this generation of youth is entering puberty at earlier ages than previous generations; girls begin hitting puberty at about age ten and above, while boys are hitting puberty at age eleven and above. Thus, boys and girls are beginning to notice (and sexually experiment with) one another at younger ages. However, a mature body does not mean that youth have developed at the same rate emotionally or mentally. Second, issues related to self-esteem and self-identification, confusion over healthy boundaries, and learning new social norms all combine to make this a complex time for young teens. And third, although younger youth enjoy spending time with the opposite sex, they are often unsure of what to do when they are together.

We're JUST Friends

Theology and the Topic

A number of Scripture passages define what it means to be a godly man or woman. Some of these passages are controversial, laughable, or highly relevant depending on the way you choose to read the Scriptures. Popular religious books for youth quote these verses as if they explain everything one needs to know about being a "man or woman of God."

However, these Scriptures (such as Ephesians 5:22-33) are too often quoted with little reference to the culture of the original audience. Without seriously explaining what "wives should submit to their husbands in everything" (Ephesians 5:24) means, youth can receive a warped idea of what it means to be a man or a woman and how the sexes should interact. Second, these Scriptures don't help youth to learn what our gender has to do with our relationship with God.

We need to help youth understand that as humans created in the image of God, we have both masculine and feminine qualities. Today's culture regularly feeds teens highly stereotyped definitions of what it is to be a male or a female. In stark contrast, the Bible is filled with diverse metaphorical language that helps us to understand the nature of God. Exploring the various male and female images of God in Scripture helps us discover who we were created to be. And since males and females tend to relate to God in different ways, our friendships with one another ultimately help us to learn about God through our differing experiences of God.

You and the Scripture

Read **Romans 12:9-21** from your favorite translation.

Often a passage is so familiar to us that it's difficult to hear it with new ears. This week's Scripture might be such a passage for you. Read the text in your favorite translation one verse at a time, then read the same verse from the translation below. After each verse, meditate on *your* translation—that is, the way this Scripture is lived out in your life.

Romans 12:9-21

[9] Love from the center of who you are; don't fake it. Run for dear life from evil; hold on for dear life to good. [10] Be good friends who love deeply; practice playing second fiddle.

[11] Don't burn out; keep yourselves fueled and aflame. Be alert servants of the Master, cheerfully expectant. Don't quit in hard times; pray all the harder. [13] Help needy Christians; be inventive in hospitality.

[14] Bless your enemies; no cursing under your breath. [15] Laugh with your happy friends when they're happy; share tears when they're down. [16] Get along with each other; don't be stuck-up. Make friends with nobodies; don't be the great somebody.

[17] Don't hit back; discover beauty in everyone. [18] If you've got it in you, get along with everybody. [19] Don't insist on getting even; that's not for you to do. "I'll do the judging," says God. "I'll take care of it."

[20] Our Scriptures tell us that if you see your enemy hungry, go by that person lunch, or if he's thirsty, get him a drink. Your generosity will surprise him with goodness. [21] Don't let evil get the best of you; get the best of evil by doing good.

Good Friends

We're JUST Friends

Scripture: Romans 12:9-21

Take—Home Learning: Friendships with members of the opposite sex are appropriate and don't have to lead to dating. Through these relationships we learn how to understand and treat others.

 indicates key activity. If time is limited, focus here.

activity	time	preparation	supplies
get ready			
Let's Get Personal	5–8 minutes	Prepare the Personal Ad Guidelines chart.	large sheet of paper, markers
jump in			
I Want to Know What Love Is	3–5 minutes	Research the meaning of the word *philadelphia*.	large sheet of paper, marker
Dear Abigail	8–12 minutes	No preparation needed.	writing paper, pens
look for life			
Let's Get Personal, the Sequel	8–10 minutes	No preparation needed.	extra Bibles, writing paper, pens
go with god			
QTJ—Quiet Time Journaling	6–8 minutes	Obtain soft background music to play during journaling.	meditative music tape/CD, students journals, pens
Rooted and Grounded in Love or Your Best Friend	5–6 minutes	Prepare two leaves per person. On a tree branch write the words "Friends of the Opposite Sex." Record "Friends" theme song.	two leaves per person, tape, tape/CD player, recorded song

Provide large sheets of paper and markers.

Before the session, write the following on a large sheet of paper.

Personal Ad Guidelines
• Interests and Abilities
• Physical appearance
• Personality description
• Time requirements
• Financial expectations
• Activities you expect to do together
• Hoped-for length of relationship
• Turn-offs and unacceptable behaviors
• Hopes for how the relationship will develop
• (Anything else you feel is important)

Jump In

Provide a large sheet of paper and marker.

Provide writing paper and pens.

 Let's Get Personal (5–7 minutes)

As youth arrive, assign them to four small groups, two groups for each sex. Say, "Today you will create a personal ad for the ideal friend." Assign each group one of the following:

Girls' Group 1—   the ideal guy who is "just a friend"
Girls' Group 2—   the ideal boyfriend
Guys' Group 1—   the ideal girl who is "just a friend"
Guys' Group 2—   the ideal girlfriend

Give each group a large sheet of paper and a marker, and instruct them to use the "Personal Ad Guidelines" to design their ads. When everyone has arrived and groups have composed their ads, invite each group to read aloud and explain its personal ad.

After all the groups have shared their ads, ask the following questions:

• What are the similarities between the ideal friends and the ideal boyfriends or girlfriends?
• What are the differences?
• Where do guys and girls have the greatest differences?
• What differences do you see between a friend of the opposite sex and a friend of the same sex?

I Want to Know What Love Is (3–5 minutes)

Say: "We use the word *love* in many different ways, and not all of them mean the same thing. Let's brainstorm a list of examples."

As youth volunteer phrases that contain the word *love,* list them on a large sheet of paper. Then ask: "Do you see any ways to categorize these items by what they have in common?" (For example, similarities might be sexual/romantic love, love of an item, or love = like.)

Say: "In Jesus' day, the Greek language had five different words for love, and each word had a different meaning. The word for family or brotherly love was *philadelphia*; the word for sexual love was *eros*; and the word for Christian love was *agape*.

Dear Abigail (8–12 minutes)

Form groups of two or three, preferably same-sex groups. Give each group paper and pens.

Say: "Since we use the word *love* in so many ways, and since some people struggle with knowing how to love others, questions about relationships are extremely common." Ask, "How many of you have read an advice column on relationships?" Wait for responses, then say, "In your group, I'd like you

Good Friends

to compose a story that deals with a relationship in which one person wants the relationship to be more or different than what the other person wants. Then write the story in the form of a letter to an advice column. The story can be a real-life experience or the story can be fictional. You have three minutes to write your letter."

After three minutes, check on the groups' progress. If they need additional time, give them another minute. When the groups have completed their letters, direct them to swap stories with another group (opposite sex, if possible). Say: "You have two minutes to read the new story and develop a response based on the earlier discussion about the different kinds of love: romantic and friendship. You may either write your response or choose someone to tell it to the larger group."

When the groups have prepared their responses (written or verbal), ask for volunteers to read aloud their group's letter and response. Discuss briefly if there is interest.

 ## Let's Get Personal, the Sequel (8–10 minutes)

Distribute Bibles to those who need them and ask everyone to locate Romans 12:9-21. Say: "In this passage, Paul is speaking to new Christians and explaining the basics of how they should act and ways they should treat one another. These verses describe the desired characteristics for all our relationships, including those with the opposite sex. Let's read the passage together as if we're encouraging one another to follow Paul's instructions."

Read the passage in unison. Ask, "Are there any phrases in this passage that you don't understand?" Consider reading the passage in different translations if there is time.

Say: "Gather with your original small group to write a revised personal ad based on this Scripture passage. Determine what new qualifications you would add as well as any you might subtract. You can make your ad serious or humorous as long as you base your ideas on this passage in Romans. You have four minutes to create a new ad."

Distribute paper and pens; help the groups if necessary. When everyone has finished, ask for volunteers to read aloud the revised personal ads.

After all the groups have read their ads, ask:
- What qualifications/requirements did you change in your new ad?
- Would it be easier or harder to find someone who fits your new ad? Why?
- If you found someone who met the requirements of your new ad, do you think your relationship would be stronger than with someone who met the qualifications of the first ad? Why or why not?

Look for Life

Provide Bibles, writing paper, and pens.

We're JUST Friends

Go With God

Provide two tree leaves and a marker per person, tape, recording of theme from "Friends" television show.

Mark one of the branches on the tree with the words, "Friends of the Opposite Sex."

 QTJ—Quiet Time Journaling (6–8 minutes)

Distribute Bibles, student journals, writing paper, and pens. Direct the students to pages 24–27 in the journal to follow the instructions there.

AND

Rooted and Grounded in Love (6 minutes)

Distribute two leaves and a marker to each person. Say: "Each week we've been adding to our tree as a visual reminder of the ways we can grow more like Jesus in our relationships. On one or both leaves, write a fact or truth that you have learned today or a verse you think is important to remember about good relationships with members of the opposite sex. Tape the leaves to the branch that reads 'Friends of the Opposite Sex.' As you attach the leaves, pray silently that your actions and attitudes toward your friends of the opposite sex will always please God."

AND/OR

Your Best Friend

Before the session, record the opening theme to the television show *Friends* or locate the *Friends* soundtrack CD. Say: "Most of you have probably heard this song before, but this time as you listen to it, I'd like you to imagine that God is singing it to you—especially the chorus. God is a friend who is always waiting and hoping to be your *best* friend." Play the song as the youth listen in silence.

Someone Special

Topic: Dating and Intimacy

Scripture: 1 Corinthians 13

Key Verse: Love is patient; love is kind; love is not envious or boastful or arrogant or rude. It does not insist on its own way; it is not irritable or resentful. (1 Corinthians 13:4-5)

Take—Home Learning: Intimacy is not a magic moment but a process that grows over a lifetime. Dating is one expression of intimacy that depends on both emotional readiness and parental support.

Younger Youth and This Topic

*Will she think I'm cool? Is he looking at me? Do I look like a complete idiot in this outfit? Why in the world did I just say **that**?* These are just some thoughts common to younger youth who desperately want to make a good impression on members of the opposite sex. Fortunately, youth often feel less of this type pressure within the safety of their peer group.

Speculation and conversation about who likes them or who thinks they're cute is normal and constant for teenagers. In fact, when that hoped-for relationship becomes a reality, it's not unusual for the *talking about* the relationship to take up more time than the relationship itself. At this age, most relationships are typically brief, lasting only a few days; yet, in that time, the courtship can be just as mesmerizing for their friends as for those involved. Teens often want to "go out" sooner than their parents allow because usually status and popularity accompanies dating. Therein lies part of the problem.

Even though younger teens may seem bright and mature, they are at a stage of rapid development (emotionally, physically, and intellectually), and they are highly vulnerable and unsure about appropriate behavior with members of the opposite sex. Typically, younger teens feel anxiety and discomfort when they are alone in a dating situation. Group interactions, such as birthday parties or movie nights, offer a safer format to practice interaction with members of the opposite sex. And though younger youth fear they'll be the last teens on earth allowed to date, there's time ahead for them to develop dating relationships.

Here are additional reasons for delaying dating: First, the time younger teens spend with same-sex peers is crucial to their development; it's likely that this time will be prematurely reduced if a steady male/female

Leader's Guide

relationship develops. Second, teenage girls (and occasionally boys) who mature faster (physically) than their peers are more likely to date someone older and, consequently, are exposed to pressures and behaviors common to the older peer group. Third, early dating—especially steady dating—has been statistically linked to a higher incidence of early sexual behavior.

While you don't set the rules for when the youth in your class should and shouldn't date, you are in a position to help them process their emotions. In addition, you can help them understand that there are many ways to express intimacy, not all of which are appropriate for every age. Be frank about the ways your own intimacy with others has grown over time as well as how you learned to make appropriate decisions in the context of relationships.

Theology and the Topic

God created us to be relational and sexual people. These capacities are marvelous gifts. During the middle school/junior high years, the realities of these gifts begin to intersect and consume our thoughts. Teens who formerly couldn't stand being around members of the opposite sex suddenly spend a lot of time talking about them, grooming themselves to be attractive to others, and worrying about their own bodies. While all of this is normal adolescent behavior, often the church responds with bewilderment and embarrassment or warnings about "sexual sin." The church urgently needs to help youth develop their own theology of sexuality.

Here are some facts youth need to learn at this point in their lives:

- In God's eyes, I'm a perfect creation. I'm OK the way I am (even when I don't see myself that way).
- Sexuality is God's gift and finds its greatest depth within the marriage relationship.
- The way I treat others—on a date or any other time—matters to God.
- At this stage, dating as preparation for the covenant of marriage is not the primary concern. Rather, dating is about discovering how to live in relationship with others and who God has created us to be.
- Dating is also a great way to practice down-to-earth spirituality through the cultivation of kindness, humility, caring, and trust.

You and the Scripture

In biblical times, individuals waited until they reached an appropriate age for marriage; then the family (to a large extent) determined a man or woman's mate. In today's society, fifteen years or more may pass between the time a person begins dating and when he or she marries.

This session looks at love—particularly the biblical concept of love—and applies it to relationships. First Corinthians 13 is used in many weddings, but it is not explicitly a passage about marriage or even love between the sexes. Read it now, and hear it as the Corinthians did—as praise for something greater than the spiritual gifts they deemed most important. Read it again as encouragement to choose the way of love over other alternatives.

One activity in this session invites youth to transform their impressions of **1 Corinthians 13** into some art form. Do the activity now by creating a poem, drawing, song, or other expression of this beautiful Scripture.

Good Friends

Someone Special

Scripture: 1 Corinthians 13

Take—Home Learning: Intimacy is not a magic moment but a process that grows over a lifetime. Dating is one expression of intimacy that depends on both emotional readiness and parental support.

 Indicates key activity. If time is limited, focus here.

activity	time	preparation	supplies
get ready			
I ♡ U or Common Language	5–7 minutes 4–6 minutes	Obtain candy hearts with messages, or use stickers. No preparation needed.	Candy hearts or stickers with words; paper, markers large sheet of paper, marker
jump in			
Common Questions	7–10 minutes	Duplicate What Do You Think? questions (page 54) before cutting apart. Obtain bowls.	two medium-sized, opaque bowls, small colored paper squares, handouts
Intimacy Grid	12–15 minutes	Duplicate Intimacy Grid (page 55). Prepare Intimacy equation chart.	large sheets of paper, markers, pens, handouts
look for life			
Love Expressed	6–8 minutes	Duplicate Expressions of Love handout (page 54). Obtain a variety of craft supplies.	a variety of craft supplies, Bibles, handouts
QTJ—Quiet Time Journaling	6–8 minutes	Obtain soft, background music to play during journaling.	meditative music tape/CD, student journals, pens
go with god			
Rooted and Grounded in Love or True Love	3–4 minutes 1–2 minutes	Prepare two tree leaves per person. On one tree branch write the words "Dating and Intimacy."	two leaves per person, markers, tape

Get Ready!

Provide small candy hearts with messages (the type you see at Valentines), sheets of paper, and markers for each table. (If you can't find candy hearts, you can use stickers with words or phrases printed on them.)

Provide a large sheet of paper and a marker.

Jump In

Provide What Do You Think? questions (page 54), two medium-sized, opaque bowls, and seven or eight each of different color, small squares of paper.

Cut apart the questions, fold them, and place them in one bowl. Shuffle the colored paper squares and place them in the second bowl.

On a large sheet of paper, write this equation: Intimacy ≠ sex.

I ♡ U (5–7 minutes)

Place a handful of candy hearts on each table, as well as a sheet of paper and a marker. Direct the youth to work in teams of three or four to compose a story about the ideal date using the words and phrases on the candy hearts. Encourage melodrama!

When the teams have finished, invite someone from each group to read aloud the group's story with as much energy and enthusiasm as possible.

OR

Common Language (4–6 minutes)

Say: "It's been a while since I was your age, so I want to make sure we can speak a common language. Explain to me some of the common phrases and activities that are associated with dating for your group."

Allow youth to lead the discussion while you listen carefully. Write on a large sheet of paper significant phrases or words. Clarify what the teens mean by such terms as *going out, dating,* or *girlfriend/boyfriend*. If students don't volunteer the information, ask questions to draw out responses. Ask: "What do you think is a common or appropriate date for young people your age? At what age do students typically begin to date in your schools?"

⚷ Common Questions (7–10 minutes)

Say: "This bowl contains several discussion questions. As we go around the room, I'd like each of you to take a question and answer it. Here's the twist, though. I also want each of you to pick one of the colored papers from this second container. Each color represents a different point of view. [*Color one*] means you answer from your own point of view. [*Color two*] means you answer as if you were the parent of a youth your age. [*Color three*] means you answer as if you were a member of the opposite sex who is your age. After you state your answer, others may agree or disagree with you and explain their reasons."

Ask for volunteers to answer the questions. Hold bowls so they can't see the questions or colors they choose. Spend only a minute or so on each question. Answer as many as time allows (don't try to answer all of them).

AND

⚷ Intimacy Grid (12–15 minutes)

Say: "People of all ages are confused about the intimacy issue. Many think if you've had sex with someone, you've achieved intimacy with that person. Or, they believe the way to be intimate with someone is to have sex with him or her, or at least to be more physical in the relationship." (Call attention to the chart and explain the equation if necessary.)

Good Friends

Continue: "Intimacy is much more than sex. Intimacy between people is expressed in caring, openness, honesty, and trust." Distribute the Intimacy Grid handouts, then say: "This is an intimacy grid. With it you will determine how various actions have different levels of intimacy, as well as how intimacy changes over time. You'll be working together to decide in which quadrant and where in that quadrant each of the actions belongs by determining where it falls on the spectrum between appropriate and inappropriate and emotional and physical. You might decide a particular action could be in more than one area depending on the circumstances. If that's the case, decide in which section it usually belongs."

Provide Intimacy Grid handout (page 55), pencils or pens.

Continue: "Intimacy can be expressed in many ways between two persons. Let's try an example. Imagine that you are a high school couple. Where on the grid would you place 'close dancing' "?

Form five groups or pairs. Assign each group one of the following type couples: seventh graders; high school seniors; married 25-year-olds; single 35-year-olds. Each group member will have a grid, however, group members may not always agree. Allow each member to complete his own grid, but instruct groups to reach a consensus regarding their assignments and to reproduce a large grid to share with the entire group. Give each group a large sheet of paper and a marker. Also instruct groups to choose one group member to report on the group's grid. Allow about six minutes for the youth to work on their grids.

If your class has fewer than eight youth, either form fewer groups or work together as one group.

When the groups have finished, compare the different grids. Ask:

• What similarities do you notice between the grids?
• What differences do you observe?
• How do you think intimacy changes over time?
• What are some ways dating can build or hurt intimacy between two persons?

Love Expressed (8–10 minutes)

Ask: "Why do you think most music, movies, and television shows deal with relationships and love?"

Look for Life

Provide Expressions of Love handout (page 54), extra Bibles, and a variety of craft supplies.

Distribute Bibles to those who need them, then ask everyone to locate 1 Corinthians 13. Say: "This is one of the best-known chapters of the Bible. While it's commonly read at weddings, the passage is not just about marriage. Paul describes what he believes makes our actions and our God-given gifts useful. In his view, Corinth was corrupt and demonstrated no values; Paul wanted to define the nature of real love. Let's read aloud this passage together. I'll start and we'll go around the circle, each reading a verse. If you'd rather not read, just say, 'Pass.' "

After reading the passage together, ask:

• What part of this passage is the hardest for you to practice?
• Which verse is your favorite and why?

Someone Special

Say: "Now I'd like you to create an original expression of what 1 Corinthians 13 means to you, especially as it relates to dating. You may focus on one verse, the entire passage, or even just a few words." Distribute the Expression of Love handouts and say: "The handout lists several creative ideas. You can work by yourself, or you can choose a partner. However, you will have only about five minutes to complete this activity. After everyone has finished, I'll ask you to comment on what you've created."

Update youth on remaining time. Try to stay on schedule in order to allow time for showing, explaining, or performing each person(s) expression of love.

 QTJ—Quiet Time Journaling (6–8 minutes)

Provide Bibles, student journals, pens, and soft background music.

Distribute Bibles, student journals and pens. Say: "Each week you've spent time focusing on our topic by journaling. No one has seen what you have written. I hope you will continue to journal even though this study is ending. The purpose today is to think about ways you can show your love in your relationships with the opposite sex in a Christlike manner. You may either work where you are or find a quiet corner to write." Direct them to read and follow the instructions on pages 28-31.

Play soft, background music for approximately six minutes while youth journal. Remind them to complete the "Not Now" section in their student journals (page 31). Youth may take their journals home today.

Go With God

Provide two tree leaves and a marker per person and tape.

On one of the tree branches write the words, "Dating and Intimacy."

Send home the journals.

Rooted and Grounded in Love (3–4 minutes)

Distribute two leaves and a marker to each person. Say: "Each week we've been adding to our tree. Today is our final time to add leaves as a visual reminder of ways we can grow more like Jesus in our relationships. On one or more leaves, write a fact or truth you've learned today or a principle or Scripture verse you think is important to remember about dating and intimacy. Tape the leaves to the 'Dating and Intimacy' branch of the tree. As you attach the leaves, pray silently for help to act in ways that are pleasing to God in your dating relationships."

Conclude the study by reviewing some of the principles, Scriptures, facts, or comments regarding all types of relationships noted on the leaves. Ask everyone to touch a part of the tree. Read together Ephesians 3:17 (on the tree), substituting the word "our" for the word "your." Pray for all the teens gathered around the tree and the relationships they represent.

AND/OR

True Love

Conclude with a reading of 1 Corinthians 13. Take turns, have one reader, or read antiphonally—one group and then the other responding.

You Think Your Family Is Weird!!!

1. This farmer's wife had a son who murdered his younger brother, then denied it (Genesis 4:1-9).

2. When he was a young child, this future leader ditched his parents for three days to go hang out with a bunch of older men without telling his parents where he was going (Luke 2:41-49).

3. After a really long cruise, this good man got drunk and cursed his own grandson (Genesis 9:20-25).

4. This disciple, one of the sons of Zebedee, went with his brother James to ask Jesus to promise them the best places in heaven (Mark 10:35-40).

5. Since her father vowed to God that he would sacrifice the first person who came out of his house if God would give him victory over his enemies, this young girl died a virgin (Judges 11:30-39).

6. Jealous of the way his father unconditionally loved his youngest son, this well-behaved son refused to come celebrate when his brother finally returned home (Luke 15:22-30).

7. This woman's father made her husband-to-be wait fourteen years to marry her and tricked her into marrying her older sister first (Genesis 29:16-28).

8. Unfortunately, the numerous sons born to this man's wives caused him great trouble because of their jealousy of one another, including rape (2 Samuel 13:14), murder (2 Samuel 13:28), rebellion (2 Samuel 15:13), and greed (1 Kings 1:5-6).

9. This mostly successful leader had seventy sons by his many wives, but the son he had with his concubine proved to be the worst. He ended up killing all but one of his half-brothers (Judges 8:29-30; 9:1-5).

10. At her mother's urging, this girl asked for the head of John the Baptist to be given to her on a plate as a present (Matthew 14:6-11).

Proverbs in Pieces

Proverbs 29:1— One who is often reproved | yet remains stubborn

will suddenly be broken beyond healing.

Proverbs 18:4—The words of the mouth | are deep waters; the fountain of

wisdom is a gushing stream.

Proverbs 25:11— A word fitly spoken

is like apples of gold in a setting of silver.

Proverbs 12:15— Fools think | their own way is right,

but the wise listen to advice.

Proverbs 15:22— Without counsel, | plans go wrong,

but with many advisers they succeed.

Proverbs 19:20— Listen to advice | and accept instruction,

that you may gain wisdom for the future.

Proverbs 24:5-6— Wise warriors are mightier than strong ones,

and those who have knowledge | than those who have strength.

Proverbs 9:9— Give instruction to the wise,

and they will become wiser still;

teach the righteous and they will gain in learning.

Will You Be My Mentor?

Follow these suggestions to make a good impression on a potential mentor.

DO:

- Look your best. While you don't have to wear your best outfit, choose something that shows you care about yourself.
- Be positive. Demonstrating a positive attitude about yourself will help you communicate that you are a likable and interesting person.
- Be honest. It's OK to identify areas/situations with which you need the most help.
- Go prepared. Take a notebook and pen with you so that you can write down phone numbers, meeting times, questions you want to ask, and so on.
- Be polite. Use titles like Mr. or Ms. if you are not normally on a first-name basis with the adult.
- Be confident. Look the potential mentor in the eye.

Don't:

- Be afraid. The person with whom you are meeting will be honored by your request to be your mentor, and chances are good that he or she will say yes.
- Be nervous. Pauses in the conversation are OK; they are a normal part of the way we communicate. If you're not sure how to comment or answer, you can always reply, "May I think about that for a while?"
- Be too brief or too talkative. One- or two-word answers may imply that you aren't able to hold up your end of the conversation. Likewise, if you talk too much, you may convey the impression that you aren't a good listener.

A Sample Script

Do you ever have a hard time saying just the right words when you are talking with an adult? If so, here's an example of dialogue to use with your potential mentor. Talk with the adult in person rather than over the phone.

"Mr./Mrs./Ms. (person's name), do you have a few minutes to talk about something?"
(If so, continue; if not, say, "Can I make an appointment with you for a time when you would be available?") "I'm looking for a mentor, and I think you'd make a great one. Could you meet with me for (one hour a week, every other week, or whatever will help you reach your goals)?

"I'm looking for a mentor because (describe to the person your goals or your reason for wanting a mentor). I'd like you to be my mentor because you (list qualities that you think would make this person a good mentor).

"Is this something you'd be willing to do, or do you have questions you'd like to ask me before you decide?"

If he or she asks to think about it for a while, say, "That would be fine. I'll call you in a few days to see what you've decided."

If she or he says no, say, "That's OK. I appreciate your being willing to think about being my mentor. Can you suggest someone else?"

If he or she says yes, say, "That's great! I look forward to working with you. Can we set up a time for our first meeting?"

Instructions for the Team

Duplicate these Scripture verses, cut apart, and place inside the tennis-ball can or other container. Use according to the instructions on page 28.

- Romans 12:9: Let love be genuine; hate what is evil, hold fast to what is good.

- Romans 12:10: Love one another with mutual affection; outdo one another in showing honor.

- Romans 12:11: Do not lag in zeal, be ardent in spirit, serve the Lord.

- Romans 12:12: Rejoice in hope, be patient in suffering, persevere in prayer.

- Romans 12:13: Contribute to the needs of the saints; extend hospitality to strangers.

- Romans 12:14: Bless those who persecute you; bless and do not curse them.

- Romans 12:15: Rejoice with those who rejoice, weep with those who weep.

- Romans 12:16: Live in harmony with one another; do not be haughty, but associate with the lowly; do not claim to be wiser than you are.

- Romans 12:17: Do not repay anyone evil for evil, but take thought for what is noble in the sight of all.

- Romans 12:18: If it is possible, so far as it depends on you, live peaceably with all.

- Philippians 2:1: If then there is any encouragement in Christ, any consolation from love, any sharing in the spirit, any compassion and sympathy... .

- Philippians 2:2: Make my joy complete: be of the same mind, having the same love ... .

- Philippians 2:2: Being in full accord and of one mind.

- Philippians 2:3: Do nothing from selfish ambition or conceit, but in humility regard others as better than yourselves.

- Philippians 2:4: Let each of you look not to your own interests, but to the interests of others.

Bitter or Better Scenarios

1. It's 8:00 at night. You've been blowing off your homework until now but decide to get started. You crack open your notebook and realize there's a project due tomorrow that you'd completely forgotten. To do the project, you need some supplies from the store. Your parents won't be home until about 10, though they do have their cell phone with them. What do you do?

- -

2. While you're walking toward your seat in the lunch room, a classmate you've never gotten along with very well intentionally trips you, causing you to spill your food. The same person then remarks to friends at the table that you are "two fries short of a Happy Meal." How do you respond?

- -

3. A teacher accuses you of breaking a demonstration model in science class (it was at the station where you usually work on your experiments, and you had been playing with it two days before). You know you didn't break it, and you have no idea how it got broken, but the teacher insists that you're lying. What do you say to the teacher?

- -

4. You've been dating someone for a few weeks, and nearly everyone in school knows it. But at a party you are unable to attend, someone tries to convince your boyfriend/girlfriend to break up with you and date him or her instead. What do you do when you hear about it?

- -

5. The girlfriend of a new member of your youth group breaks up with him. She also is a member of the group and a close friend of yours. When he attends the next youth event, several people accuse him of coming just because she's there. He is offended by these comments and strongly denies they are true. Should you get involved in the conflict? How?

- -

6. Your younger brother by two years has been getting on your nerves lately. In addition to making a lot of rude comments about your friends, he also has been teasing you about your body and your zits. Today you catch him snooping around your room, rummaging through your stuff. What's your immediate reaction?

- -

7. Your friend has a bad habit of not returning the stuff you lend her. Today you tell her that you absolutely need your favorite CD to take with you on a weekend trip. She says: "Oh, I've been meaning to tell you. I lost it about three weeks ago when I was at a party, and I don't know where it is now." What do you say to her?

- -

8. One of your friends tells you that another of your good friends has been spreading hurtful lies about you. The next time you see this alleged rumor-spreader, what do you do?

- -

9. You're with a bunch of friends in a fast-food restaurant, talking and enjoying the free refills. The restaurant is moderately busy though certainly not full. As the noise level in the restaurant rises, the level of your group's conversation increases also. An employee comes over to your table and sternly says, "You're going to have to leave now." What do you say to him or her in return?

What Do You Think?

- What is an appropriate date for an eighth grader?

- What is the purpose of dating?

- What's the difference between intimacy and love?

- How do the expectations of guys and girls differ when it comes to relationships?

- Does dating at an early age make you more likely to have sex at an early age?

- What is the most important quality to look for in a potential date?

- What is the most important quality for you to have if you want to attract others?

- Is it wrong to date someone only because you like his or her looks?

- What is the best age for a person to start dating?

- Do you have to be physical to be intimate?

- Does having sex with someone mean you experience intimacy with him or her?

First Corinthians Thirteen: Expressions of Love

Here are some ideas to get you started:

- Write a poem to a date based on a portion of this chapter.
- Create a skit that demonstrates how you could live out this passage on a date.
- Make a clay model or drawing of how this passage makes you feel.
- Write the passage using creative lettering in the shape of a heart.

- Think of one of your favorite songs about love. How does it measure up to this passage?
- Write a prayer to God in which you express your feelings about dating.
- Begin composing a song that uses the words from this chapter.
- Read a Bible commentary on this passage and see if you can learn more about what this passage means.

Intimacy Grid

Instructions:

(1) Check which group your grid is for:
_____ Seventh graders
_____ High school seniors
_____ Married 25-year-olds
_____ Single 35-year-olds

(2) In light of your assigned group (above), determine together the location on the grid below of each of the acts of intimacy. Place its number in the quadrant that represents your decision as to the appropriateness of the act. For example, if something is emotionally appropriate, you would place its number in the upper left square. If it were physically inappropriate, you would place its number in the lower right square.

Acts of Intimacy

1. Giving a hug around the shoulder
2. Giving a full body hug
3. Kissing on the cheek
4. Kissing quick on the lips
5. Kissing long or passionately on the lips
6. Touching above the waist
7. Touching below the waist
8. Having sex
9. Sharing a secret
10. Sharing your hopes and dreams for the future
11. Going on a group date
12. Going on a date alone
13. Holding hands
14. Talking about what turns you on sexually
15. Seeing each other naked
16. Giving a back rub

EMOTIONAL	PHYSICAL
APPROPRIATE	APPROPRIATE
NOT APPROPRIATE	NOT APPROPRIATE
PHYSICAL	EMOTIONAL

Great Friends: A Retreat

Retreats are ideal for building and nurturing relationships among youth and youth and leaders. Retreats also provide opportunity to spend concentrated time on a particular subject area. Although this retreat focuses on the topic of relationships, the format may be adjusted to suit any topic or situation.

For a complete list of supplies needed during the retreat, see page 59.

Sample Schedule Friday

6:30 Dinner

7:30 Leave for Retreat

8:30 Get Acquainted

9:30 Large Group Activity

9:45 It's in the Cards

Friday

Meet at a local fast-food restaurant for dinner. Arrange for adequate leaders/parents to transport youth, other leaders, overnight bags, sleeping bags, and so on. If your budget allows, pay for everyone's meal; otherwise, be sure to announce ahead of time that youth will pray for their own dinners.

Before leaving the restaurant, give everyone an index card and a pen. Instruct each person to choose a partner and to identify ten ways the restaurant demonstrated itself to be customer-friendly and service-oriented. Collect the cards and save them for later use.

Once everyone arrives at the retreat locations, allow for some free time. Plan a few get-acquainted or group-building games. Borrow game books from your church's youth ministry library, or research games online at *www.youthpastor.com*.

After settling in, distribute the index cards you previously collected at the restaurant. (It doesn't matter if some youth get their own cards.) On one large sheet of paper, list all the ways the youth noticed the restaurant was customer-friendly. On another large sheet of paper, list the ways they were service-oriented.

Say: "Restaurants must remember they are in business to make their customers happy, or else they probably won't be too successful."

Ask:
• What similarities do you see between what a restaurant does to please its customers and what we can do to enjoy good relationships with others?
• What differences do you see?

Say: "A restaurant's mission is to take care of and to serve others. How is that mission similar to our calling as Christians?"

Play **It's in the Cards from Session Two** (page 16). Allow youth additional time to build their house of cards. Also, rather than limiting the conversation to friendships, ask youth to name actions/attitudes that build good relationships with others.

Complete **Friendship Killers and Keepers from Session Two** (page 16). Modify the instructions by asking youth to discuss Relationship Killers and Keepers.

Conclude the Friday night session with music and a closing prayer. Include at least one song about relationships, such as "They'll Know We Are Christians by Our Love."

Allow free time or encourage friendly competition during a group board-game session.

Power Failure

Saturday

Distribute student journals, and direct youth to find a quiet spot where they can be alone with God. Explain that they have thirty minutes to read their devotions, to reflect, and to pray. They can work on any of the devotions in the journal or revisit ones they have previously completed during class sessions.

Form groups of six to eight and play **Are You a Wise One? from Session Three** (page 22). The game will be easier to play with small groups than with one large group. Following are additional proverbs about relationships for use in the game:

Arab proverb: "Examine what is said ..." (not the one who speaks).
Czech proverb: "Do not protect yourself by a fence, but rather by ..." (your friends).

Danish proverb: "God gives every bird its food, but does not ..." (always drop it into the nest).

Estonian proverb: "Where you find fault with something ..." (come and give a hand.)

Greek proverb: "The heart that loves ..." (is always young.)

Japanese proverb: "A single arrow is easily broken, but ..." (not ten in a bundle).

Korean proverb: "A stranger nearby is better than ..." (a far-away relative).

Romanian proverb: "If you wish good advice ..." (consult an old man).

Russian proverb: "Tell me who's your friend and I'll ..." (tell you who you are).

Swedish proverb: "Go often to the house of a friend, for ..." (weeds soon choke up the unused path).

Note: Proverbs came from the same website as the ones in the session:
tp://cogweb.ucla.edu/Discourse/Proverbs/Miscellaneous.html

Great Friends: A Retreat

10:00 Friendship Killers and Keepers

10:20 Music and Prayer

11:00 Free Time

12:00 Lights Out

Saturday

8:00 Breakfast

9:00 Devotions

9:30 Are You a Wise One?

After reading each proverb, discuss what meaning the youth understand in the proverb and what that meaning has to do with relationships.

Say: "Last night we identified some things that build and tear apart our relationships with others. We're going to read two Scripture passages that give us instructions for our life on the Christian team."

10:30 Instructions for the Team

Complete the **Instructions for the Team activity from Session Four** (page 29).

11:00 Recreation

Lead a group recreation activity (such as volleyball, softball), or allow free time

12:00 Lunch

If your group is large and many of the youth don't know one another, consider having a random drawing to determine who will sit at each table.

1:30 I'm Lichen It!

Conduct **I'm Lichen It! from Session Four** (page 28) followed by a Cooperatively Planned Game Event. Form small groups of two or three. Provide each group a game or activity planning resource, such as a youth ministry idea resource. Explain that they have twenty minutes to choose or invent and plan the "all-time greatest" activity that illustrates the ideas learned in the I'm Lichen It! activity—cooperation, depending on others, symbiosis, and so on. Youth are limited to the resources and supplies they can collect during the time allowed. After twenty minutes, direct each group to lead in its game or activity.

At the conclusion of the all-time greatest activities, provide extended free time. In case of inclement weather, provide board games, card games, or a movie that deals with relationships. (See the Out and About Progressive Movie Lock-in on page 60 for movie tips.)

5:30 Dinner

Direct youth to pair up with a friend before sitting and eating with a different pair who they may not know as well.

6:30 Love Is/Love Isn't

Read together 1 Corinthians 13. Divide a large sheet of paper into two columns; write "Love Is" on the left side and "Love Isn't" on the right side. Invite youth to review the verses in the passage and identify the descriptions of love that belong under each heading.

Say: "Take about five minutes to look through your CDs. What can you find that does and doesn't meet the love standards outlined in this Bible passage. We'll listen to and talk about as many of the songs as we can."

After the youth have spent a few minutes finding clips that do or do not meet the real love criteria spelled out in 1 Corinthians 13, invite volunteers to play their song clips or read aloud the words. Discuss the lyrics when there is interest.

Good Friends

Sit in a circle. If your group is larger than about fifteen people, you may wish to form two groups. Give each person a safety pin (approximately one inch long), as well as one color of embroidery floss and a pair of scissors. Say: "Cut the embroidery thread into three-inch-long pieces (about the length of your longest finger). Cut as many pieces as there are persons in this room."

Once everyone has cut their pieces of thread, collect the scissors. Say: "One of the ways we can demonstrate our love for one another is to build them up by complimenting them. One at a time, we will pass our pins around the circle. When a pin comes to you, tell one attribute you appreciate about the person whose pin you have, and tie one of your threads around the bottom part of his or her pin (not the part that opens). It's OK to say something that another person has already said, as long as you are naming qualities or talents you truly like in the person."

Begin with the person who's had the most recent birthday, then move to his or her left until all youth have passed around their pins. Ask teens to wear the pins for the remainder of the retreat. Close with a group hug and a simple prayer of thanks for the many gifts and friendships represented in the group.

Show a movie with a relationship theme. See the "Progressive Movie Lock-in" for discussion instructions.

Power Failure

Sunday

The retreat has focused on the different relationships in our lives. Use the I Call You My Friends worship program (page 63) to conclude and emphasize that Christians are connected because of their love for one another through God.

Supplies Needed for Retreat

__ student journals
__ index cards
__ pens or pencils
__ CD player
__ several decks of cards
__ safety pins (one- and one-half inch)
__ embroidery thread in multiple colors
__ several pairs of scissors
__ several large sheets of paper
__ markers
__ handouts
__ board games
__ youth ministry resources/games
__ vcr/tv

7:30 Friendship Pins

This activity takes a good chunk of time, but the youth appreciate hearing the positive comments about themselves and others.

9:30 Movie Time

12:00 Lights Out

Sunday

8:00 Breakfast

9:00 Pack and Clean Up

9:30 Worship

10:30 Depart

Out and About: Progressive Movie Lock—in

Topic: Relationships in the Movies

Leader Instructions:

- Prior to the lock-in, remember to research and obtain any required license for viewing movies in public settings. Note information at the bottom of this page.

- Preview any movies you choose to show.

Here's a simple, easy-to-plan movie lock-in that you can easily tailor to the needs of your youth. Just follow these step-by-step instructions, add a bit of your own ingenuity, and you'll soon create a fun lock-in or daylong retreat that can easily be repeated at a later date.

1. *Decide on the date and time of your lock-in.* Twelve to fourteen hours is probably a good time span. Ideas for scheduling are from Friday at 6 P.M. until Saturday at 8 A.M., or you consider an all-day event on Saturday from 9 A.M. to 9 P.M.
2. *Choose the movies you wish to show.* Look for a variety of movie topics that deal with relationships in different ways—those between family members, high school boyfriends and girlfriends, teachers and students, teammates, and so forth. If you decide to show PG-13 movies, you may want to send a permission slip home to parents informing them of the movie choices. Here are some examples of movies to consider, but you'll want to pick movies you are familiar with and that you think are right for your youth:

- *Finding Forrester* (2000) or *Dead Poets Society* (1989) **[mentors]**
- *Bye Bye, Love* (1984) **[divorce]**
- *Can't Buy Me Love* (1987) **[dating, popularity]**
- *Father of the Bride, Part 2* (1995) **[marriage, parent/child relationships]**
- *Grease* (1978) **[friendships]**
- *Groundhog Day (1993); Romeo and Juliet* (1996 version) **[dating]**
- *Rudy* (1993) or *The Sandlot* (1993) **[teamwork]**
- *Save the Last Dance* (2001) **[Relationships portrayed in non-white culture]**
- *Liar, Liar* (1997) **[trust/lies within relationships]**
- *Stand By Me* (1986) **[friendship]**
- *The Spitfire Grill* (1996) **[forgiveness, community]**

Preview any movies you haven't viewed recently or at all. Take notes regarding how the films portray relationships. Be sure to abide by the following regulations concerning showing videos in public places:

(1) Obtain a public performance license (sometimes called a site or umbrella license) to show movies on home video publicly, even for educational purposes.
(2) A church video license can be granted by the new joint venture between Motion Picture Licensing Corporation (MPLC) and Christian Copyright Licensing International (CCLI), Christian Video Licensing International (CVLI). CVLI can be reached at 888-771-CVLI (fax 310-822-0908).
(3) Check to see whether your church or conference is already covered by a site license for public performance for video.

Good Friends

3. Choose and preview one or two movies currently showing in local theaters that deal with relationships.
4. Organize a tentative schedule, listing approximate starting times for each movie. Keep in mind that movies and times usually change on Fridays at most theaters. You probably won't be able to finalize your schedule until the day of the event.
5. Identify several locations at which to view the movies. For example, one might be at your home, another in a theater, two of them at the homes of some of the youth, and possibly two more at the church.
6. Ask host families or some of the youth to provide snacks for each location.
7. Mail a flier and permission form to parents two or three weeks in advance. Charge as small a fee as possible.
8. Recruit drivers and additional chaperones.
9. Begin the evening by saying: "Relationships are a major emphasis in most movies, because relationships are important in most human beings' lives. Over the next few hours, we're going to watch several movies that deal with different kinds of relationships. After each viewing, we'll talk about that film a bit and focus on some questions I'd like you to pay attention to during each movie."
10. Prior to the lock-in, duplicate as many copies of the questions below as you expect youth. Remember, you will provide each person a new copy of the questions before each movie begins (see below). After the group views each movie, spend about ten to fifteen minutes debriefing the film. This process will help youth to develop a framework for viewing movies with a more critical eye.
11. You may choose to supplement the discussion with one or more appropriate Scripture verses.

Progressive Movie Retreat

Questions to Think About

• What were the key relationship issues in the movie?

• What were positive or appropriate portrayals of relationships?

• What were bad, stereotypical, or inappropriate portrayals of relationships?

• Where was God in the midst of the relationships? (That is, what actions were most like how Jesus calls us to live our lives?)

• Where was God absent from or most needed in a relationship?

• What Bible story or passage does this movie bring to mind for you?

Duplicate this page so that your leader book remains intact. Using the duplicate copy, cut off these questions, then duplicate as many copies as needed for each movie discussion.

Out and About: Progressive Movie Lock-in

STUDENT MOVIE PASS

Form for Parent's or Guardian's Consent

Youth Leader: Each student in your group needs to receive a parent's or guardian's consent before viewing movies that are rated PG, PG-13, or R. Photocopy this page, fill in the Youth Leader section, and send a copy home with each student in the youth group.

For Youth Leader:

Our youth group will be viewing and discussing the religious themes of

_____ on _____ .
(name of movie)   (date)

This movie is rated _____ for:

_____

_____

✂ -

(Parents, cut apart at this line and return the signed consent form to youth leader.)

For Parent or Guardian:

I give my consent for _____ to view this
(name of youth)

movie in a supervised youth group setting.

_____
(parent's or guardian's signature)

Good Friends

Worship Service
"I Call You My Friends"

This worship service focuses on relationships and how we are connected to one another through God. Ask youth to join you on the floor, sitting in a circle. Light a candle and place it in the center of the circle.

Songs

Sing several songs about showing God's love to the world, such as "They'll Know We are Christians by Our Love."

Scripture

Ask one of the youth to read aloud John 15:12-17; or, if you can project the words on a wall or screen, read aloud the passage in unison.

Homily

Show the clip from *Wayne's World* (approximately 33:30 to 35:20) where Garth and Wayne are sitting on a car, talking about life. Discuss the ordinary friendship represented in the clip. Invite the youth to name and describe qualities that make a great friend. Conclude by making a connection to the Scripture and to Jesus being our best friend.

Prayer

Distribute pens or markers and narrow strips of colored paper. Ask: "What is a prayer chain?" If you have volunteers to respond, as one to describe a prayer chain's function. If no one responds, say: "A prayer chain is a fast method for sharing prayer concerns with others who are on a special list. Someone calls the first person on the list, passes on the message, and then that person calls the next person on the list, and so on."

Say: "We're going to create our own unique prayer chain. On each strip of paper, write a name or situation that comes to mind for the category that I mention. After you write each item, close your eyes and imagine that person or situation flooded with light and surrounded by God's love. On the [*first color*] paper, write the name of a friend about whom you're concerned. *(pause)* On the [*second color*] paper, write a phrase that describes a relationship you are in that needs healing. *(pause)* On the [*third color*] paper, write the name of a family member or an adult for whom you give God thanks. *(pause)* On the [*fourth color*] paper, write an area in which you need God's help with your relationships. *(pause)*

When everyone has finished his or her prayer strips, pass around cellophane tape or staplers. Ask participants to create paper chains using their strips, then to connect their ends with the ends of those on their right and left sides. When the entire chain is formed, ask each person to hold her or his part of the chain.

Worship Service

Provide a candle, matches, construction paper in at least four different colors, tape or staplers, and pens or pencils.

Leader Instructions:
• Ahead of time, cut four narrow strips of construction paper in four different colors for each youth/leader attending the worship service.
• If you choose to project the Scripture on the wall or screen, arrange for the necessary audiovisual equipment.

Say: "We are connected in so many ways. This circle represents the bonds we have formed with one another, bonds that are strong like a chain, but that can be easily torn apart like paper. I'd like us to pass this chain around the circle." (Direct students to work together to pass the chain to their right. When the chain has moved approximately halfway around the circle, stop.)

Say: "The Bible says teaches us to pray for one another and to carry one another's burdens. So beginning with me and going around the circle, we'll each rip off a section of four links to take home with us. Even though you may not know the people or situations written on the paper, you can still share these concerns with God in your own prayer time, and you can gain strength from knowing that someone else is praying for you."

Benediction

Ask youth to join hands, stretching out to make the largest circle possible. Then ask students to imagine that God is in the middle of the circle. As they continue to hold hands, ask them to take one or two steps toward the center of the circle—toward God. Youth will discover the closer they move toward God, the closer they are to one another. While remaining in the circle, ask them to move as close as possible to one another. Point out the obvious: that in moving closer together, they move closer to God. Conclude with a blessing such as, "Friends of Jesus, go forth and be friends to one another, friends to your families, and friends to the world. Amen."

This activity is adapted from "To Love as God Loves," Saint Dorotheos of Gaza, (Sixth Century).

Good Friends